Authors

Ulrich Wiehle
Michael Diegelmann
Henryk Deter
Dr. Peter Noel Schömig
Michael Rolf

100 IFRS Financial Ratios

ISBN 3-9809461-7-7

Author's preface

Dear readers,

in order to make solid investments, investors compare companies within their peer group. For this purpose, key ratios such as EBIT, working capital or cash flow have become increasingly important in recent years. These ratios are part of the daily business in order to measure corporate perfomance and to get an insight into a company's fundamental situation. It is therefore an important prerequisite to know a ratio's significance not only for investors to make the right decisions, but also for managers to lead a business unit into the right direction. But this reference book not only addresses investors and managers, it is also helpful for auditors, tax accountants or students to quickly refresh the know how on corporate ratios both quickly and in-depth.

For a better understanding we have added a sample calculation to each ratio's definition as well as the fields of application. A critical assessment of each financial ratio is explained by discussing both advantages and disadvantages. Please note that differences in the way of calculation may still exist, which you should be aware of.

When analyzing financial ratios, one should make sure to always compare the ratios relative to the peer-group and the industry standards, as otherwise an isolated number would have a very limited significance. Finally the key for successful research is to transfer comprehensive analysis of several indicators into a meaningful result. For this purpose the reference book delivers a strong added value!

Sincerely, your authors

E-mail your questions, remarks or feedback to: **IFRS@cometis.de**

How to use the booklet

All financial ratios described in this book have the following structure:

- Formula
- Sample calculation based on an exemplary annual report
- Explanation
- Advantages and disadvantages

Each description was thoroughly researched. Thus for each ratio we have used the formula which is regularly used in existing literature. Nevertheless there are different approaches for calculating a financial ratio (depending on the complexity), of which the user of this handbook should be aware when discussing with fund managers, auditors, bankers or rating experts.

Most of the sample calculations are based upon the year 2 of the exemplary annual report (IFRS) in chapter one (Income statement, Balance sheet, Cash flow statement). Information, which is necessary for the calculation but at the same time not part of the annual report can be found on page 17, section "Additional information".

The corresponding explanation sheds light on the composition of each ratio and its usefulness as an indicator for analyzing the company's performance. It is also explained which other ratios should be considered at the same time for making reasonable judgments of a company's economic situation. The advantages and disadvantages help the reader to question the whole purpose of a financial ratio, independent of the actual outcome.

Please be aware that due to the wide range of information available in the market, neither the form nor the extent of each financial ratio is exhaustive.

Table of content

Table of content

Table of content

Table of content

Chapter 1

Exemplary annual report

1.1   Income statement

in million EUR

Income statement	Year 2	Year 1
Sales	**14,019**	**14,226**
Cost of sales	5,004	5,178
Gross profit	**9,015**	**9,048**
Marketing and distribution costs	6,279	6,294
Research and development costs	300	279
Administrative expenses	753	780
Amortization of goodwill	90	90
Other operating income	294	288
Other operating expenses	435	477
Operating profit (EBIT)	**1,452**	**1,416**
Interest income	66	78
Interest expense	(12)	(27)
Other financial income and expenses	(9)	(33)
Earnings before tax (EBT)	**1,497**	**1,434**
Taxes	(594)	(564)
Minority interest	(21)	(21)
Net income	**882**	**849**

1.2 Balance sheet

in million EUR

Balance sheet - Assets	Year 2	Year 1
Intangible assets	291	384
Property, plant and equipment	2,736	2,751
Financial assets	66	66
Fixed assets	**3,093**	**3,201**
Inventories	2,016	2,031
Trade receivables	2,064	2,025
Other receivables and assets	282	330
Cash and cash equivalents	2,526	2,166
Current assets	**6,888**	**6,552**
Deferred taxes	84	66
Prepaid expenses and deferred charges	69	75
Total assets	**10,134**	**9,894**

1.2 Balance sheet

in million EUR

Balance sheet - Equity and liabilities	Year 2	Year 1
Share capital	645	645
Capital reserves	141	141
Retained earnings	3,789	3,486
Net income	882	849
Shareholders' equity	**5,457**	**5,121**
Minorities	36	60
Total equity	**5,493**	**5,181**
Pension provisions	1,140	1,191
Other provisions	1,437	1,533
Total provisions	**2,577**	**2,724**
Long-term debt	288	288
Trade payables	909	879
Other liabilities	468	444
Total liabilities	**1,665**	**1,611**
Deferred taxes	372	357
Deferred income	27	21
Total shareholders' equity and liabilities	**10,134**	**9,894**

1.3 Cash flow statement

in million EUR

Cash flow statement	Year 2	Year 1
EBIT	**1,452**	**1,416**
Taxes	(711)	(567)
Depreciation and amortization	492	483
Change in long-term provisions (excl. interest)	(33)	(12)
Profit/loss on disposal of non-current assets	3	3
Change in inventories	15	81
Change in trade receivables and other assets	(27)	(138)
Change in liabilities and short-term provisions	57	(90)
Cash flow from operating activities	**1,248**	**1,176**
Payments for non-current assets	(507)	(726)
Proceeds on disposal of non-current assets	33	45
Proceeds on interest, dividends and other financial income	150	120
Cash flow from investing activities	**(324)**	**(561)**
Dividends paid	(354)	(327)
Change in long-term liabilities	0	(99)
Interest and other financial expense	(141)	(126)
Cash flow from financing activities	**(495)**	**(552)**
Foreign exchange rate effects	(69)	(39)
Change in cash and cash equivalents	**360**	**24**
Cash and cash equivalents, beginning of year	2,166	2,142
Cash and cash equivalents, end of year	2,526	2,166

1.4 Additional information

No. of common shares outstanding	354.0 mn
No. of preferred shares outstanding	–
Current share price	35.00 EUR
Dividend per share	1.00 EUR
Personnel expenses	2,453 mn
Full-time employees	46,000
Capitalized R&D: Year 1 Year 2	500 mn 550 mn
Accumulated depreciation	2,650 mn
Compounded average growth rate (CAGR)	10%
Company rating/Corporate bond spread	AA/0.3%
Risk-free interest rate	4.5%
Market risk premium	3.5%

Chapter 2

Income statement ratios

2.1 EBIT

Formula	**Sample calculation**
Net income	882
± Extraordinary items	0
+ Minority interest	21
+ Taxes	594
± Financial result	(45)
= EBIT	**= 1,452**

Explanation

EBIT stands for "earnings before interest and taxes". In the US the ratio is also known as operating income/operating profit. It is generally used to assess the company's earnings position, in particular in international comparisons. However, EBIT is not only pure earnings before interest and taxes as it is referred to by many people, but in more precise terms it is the operating result before the financial and thus investment result, which may have a major impact on the pre-tax earnings depending on the respective company. EBIT can also be calculated by subtracting total operating expenses from sales (incl. other operating income).

Advantages	Disadvantages
• Allows assumptions to be made about pure operating activities	• Only meaningful when considered together with other indicators (e.g., revenues)
• Industry-wide comparisons of operating income are possible, in particular when other ratios are also considered (e.g., revenues)	• Interest income, which may not be included in EBIT, can be part of operating income (income from financing activities, e.g., financing installments)
• Distortions from tax effects are not included	• Income which may not stem from the operating activities may also be included in this figure (rental income)
• Used internationally	

2.2 EBITDA

Formula	Sample calculation
Net income	882
± Extraordinary items	0
+ Minority interest	21
+ Taxes	594
± Financial result	(45)
+ Depreciation and amortization	492
= EBITDA	**= 1,944**

Explanation

EBITDA stands for "earnings before interest, taxes, depreciation and amortization". These earnings before interest, taxes, depreciation of tangible assets and amortization of intangible assets (in particular goodwill) are cash flow like, as the write-downs not reflected in liquidity are added to the operating income in a similar manner to calculations for the indirect cash flow. EBITDA is often used as an indicator for young, high-growth companies or for companies with exceptionally high write-down requirements – these companies may also generate negative net income. Alternatively EBITDA may be calculated by subtracting total operating expenses from sales (incl. other operating income) and adding depreciation and amortization for the period.

Advantages	Disadvantages
• The impact of various forms of financing is not considered (may not apply to leasing)	• Only truly meaningful together with other indicators (e.g., EV/EBITDA)
• Write-downs have no impact	• Cross-industry comparisons are difficult
• Can be used as approximation of cash flow	• Income which cannot be directly allocated to pure operating activities (rental income) is included in the calculation
• Makes international comparison more simple, as national taxes are not included	

2.3   Earnings before taxes

Formula	Sample calculation
Net income	882
± Extraordinary items	0
+ Minority interest	21
+ Taxes	594
= Earnings before taxes (EBT)	**= 1,497**

Explanation

Earnings before taxes (or income/profit before taxes) is used as a comparative indicator for a company's earnings power in international comparisons, as income taxes are not taken into account. However, income before taxes does include financing costs, which are also subject to national tax laws and income from the disposal of assets. This in turn does restrict international comparability. Income before taxes is an indicator often used in particular in conjunction with revenues (pre-tax margin).

Advantages	Disadvantages
• Different tax regulations in various countries do not have any impact	• Only meaningful if other indicators are also considered (e.g., revenues)
• Costs of capital are, in part, not considered	• Can vary strongly over time
• Interest income which forms part of operating income (financing income) is considered	• International comparison is difficult due to the major impact of national accounting regulations reflected in this figure

2.4   Net income

Formula	Sample calculation
Sales	14,019
+ Other operating income	294
− Total operating expenses	(12,861)
± Financial result	45
− Taxes	(594)
− Minority interest	(21)
± Extraordinary items	0
= Net income	**= 882**

Explanation

Net income is the positive (otherwise: net loss) difference between income and expenses in the period under review and is thus the bottom line of the income statement. It shows a corporation's income for a period. When calculating this figure profits or losses carried forward and additions to or withdrawals from open reserves are not considered. Net income is the initial figure for calculating other important ratios such as earnings per share, return on equity or return on sales.

Advantages	Disadvantages
• Future estimates for listed companies are available (in particular based on earnings per share, if necessary after adjustment)	• International comparison not possible
• Intuitive	• Net income for the year is subject to the greatest possible accounting discretion, which in turn affects all indicators linked to net income
• Taxes and thus concrete expenses are considered	• Net income is not as meaningful as the cash flow

2.5 Financial result

Formula   **Sample calculation**

Interest income	66
+ Interest expense	(12)
± Write-downs / write-ups for financial assets	0
± Write-downs / write-ups for marketable securities	0
+ Other financial income and expenses	(9)
= Financial result	**= 45**

Explanation

The financial result is the difference between EBIT and EBT. For most industrial companies the financial result is negative, as the interest charged on borrowing generally exceeds income from investments (dividends). If a company records a positive financial result over several periods, then we must ask how much capital is invested at which interest rate, and if this capital would not bear a greater yield if it were invested in the company's growth. From an investor's perspective, a constant, positive financial result also raises the issue of a special distribution to shareholders.

Advantages	Disadvantages
• The financial result provides information about financing costs	• The financial result may include operating components (income from financing activities)
• Information may be gained about non-consolidated companies	• Investment income as a component of the financial result does not provide any information on the risk inherent in this investment
	• May vary strongly over time

2.6 Net operating profit after taxes (NOPAT)

Formula	**Sample calculation**
EBIT	1,452
+ Amortization of intangible assets	90
+ Δ Provisions	(147)
− Operating taxes	(594)
+ Interest on leasing expense	0
+ Δ Capitalized R&D expense	50
= **NOPAT**	= **851**

Explanation

NOPAT stands for net operating profit after taxes, and shows which profit the company would achieve in the event of pure equity financing. This means that NOPAT is an alternative way to measure operating success for every company which uses the leverage effect of debt capital.

In contrast to EBIT, NOPAT does not take into account the tax savings which a company generates as a result of high debt.

Advantages	**Disadvantages**
• Independent of type of financing	• Large number of adjustments possible
• Considers the pure operating result	
	• Based on accounting material, is thus less precise than cash flows as accounting standards come into play
• Taxes are taken into account as an expense	
• Leasing financing is generally adjusted	

2.7   Tax rate

Formula

$$\frac{\text{Income taxes}}{\text{Earnings before taxes}} \times 100\%$$

Sample calculation

$$\frac{594}{1,497} \times 100\% = \textbf{39.68\%}$$

Explanation

The tax rate describes the relationship between income taxes and income before taxes, in order to show the relative impact on earnings from taxation. In the global economy, the tax rate is often a key criterion when companies chose where to locate. The tax rate is, in turn, closely linked to calculating the cost of debt, as the tax shield from borrowing interest must be taken into account.

Advantages	Disadvantages
• Pertinent for use in national comparisons	• May fluctuate heavily over time
• A reasonable indicator for a company's future tax rates in relatively stable tax systems	• Losses carried forward and tax provisions make forecasting of actual future tax expense difficult
• Shows actual expense	• In the case of international groups, it is hardly possible to analytically derive future tax payments due to the immense complexity

2.8 R&D cost ratio

Formula

$$\frac{\text{Research \& Development costs}}{\text{Sales}} \times 100\%$$

Sample calculation

$$\frac{300}{14,019} \times 100\% = \textbf{2.14\%}$$

Explanation

The R&D cost ratio shows what proportion of total sales the company reinvests in research and development (R&D). As a rule, companies that work in research-intensive sectors such as pharmaceuticals or biotechnology, and whose success depends on product innovations, have higher research cost ratios. Increases to the ratio are generally linked to increased R&D investment, however they can also be caused by a slump in sales. A reduction in the research cost ratio can generally be put down to a reduction in research activities, however it may also be linked to increases in productivity and thus lower costs.

Advantages	Disadvantages
• Allows conclusions to be made about research efficiency • Offers starting points for reviewing competitive ability • Used in company comparisons	• Can sometimes not be clearly identified from the income statement • R&D costs cannot be clearly calculated (classification) • Varying R&D costs may be simpler than in other cost blocks and is used to keep to profit targets (consequence: variations in profit quality)

2.9 Cost of sales to total operating expense

Formula

$$\frac{\text{Cost of sales}}{\text{Total operating expense}} \times 100\%$$

Sample calculation

$$\frac{5,004}{12,861} \times 100\% = \textbf{38.90\%}$$

Explanation

The ratio of cost of sales to total operating expense describes the economy of material use, which is directly linked to generating revenues. When interpreting this indicator, changes in procurement prices (e.g., raw materials) and changed warehousing must be taken into account. Moreover, the ratio should be compared to total sales.

The higher the ratio of cost of sales to total operating expense, the stronger the impact a reduction in this indicator would be on the company's earnings. This can be achieved, for example, by relocating purchasing to regions with a lower cost structure or by exploiting currency advantages. This ratio should always be considered in conjunction with product quality, i.e., companies should not aim to reduce the ratio at any expense.

Advantages	Disadvantages
• Good indicator for competitive comparisons	• Highly industry dependent
• Indicates productivity (in combination with ratio of personnel expense to total operating expense)	• Dependent on procurement market
• Key indicator, as cost of sales is generally one of the company's largest expense items	

2.10 Depreciation and amortization to total operating expense

Formula

$$\frac{\text{Depreciation and amortization}}{\text{Total operating expense}} \times 100\%$$

Sample calculation

$$\frac{492}{12,861} \times 100\% = \textbf{3.83\%}$$

Explanation

The ratio of depreciation and amortization to total operating expense indicates how efficiently the assets employed are being used. If this ratio increases, this generally leads to increased profits being disclosed in subsequent years. A high ratio of depreciation and amortization to total operating expense may also indicate that a company has an aggressive investment policy.

In contrast, a low level of depreciation and amortization may indicate outdated assets that offer opportunities for new investments and rationalization or increases in productivity.

Advantages	Disadvantages
• Indicates degree of rationalization regarding total costs • Highly meaningful in conjunction with ratios of personnel and material expense to total operating expense • Recognition of productivity potential	• Difficult to calculate, as amortization and depreciation expense is heavily affected by accounting policy • Highly industry-dependent • Highly dependent on investing activities

2.11 Depreciation and amortization to sales

Formula

$$\frac{\text{Depreciation and amortization}}{\text{Sales}} \times 100\%$$

Sample calculation

$$\frac{492}{14,019} \times 100\% = \mathbf{3.51\%}$$

Explanation

The ratio depreciation and amortization to total sales indicates what portion of total revenue was written-off. As a rule, write-downs only include depreciation of property, plant and equipment and amortization of intangible assets (e.g., goodwill), but not extraordinary write-downs for financial assets or depreciation of low-value assets.

An increase in this ratio can result from new investments that are not yet reflected in sales figures or may result from the formation of hidden assets. A falling ratio can be an indicator for a falling readiness to make investments.

Advantages	Disadvantages
• Excellent information on productivity (consumption of economic assets per unit of sales)	• Depends on write-down methody
	• Highly industry-dependent
• Used in sector comparisons	• Artificial improvement through reduced reinvestment
• Used in analyses over time	

2.12 Write-down structure

Formula

$$\frac{\text{Type of write-down}}{\text{Depreciation and amortization}} \times 100\%$$

Sample calculation

Here: goodwill amortization

$$\frac{90}{492} \times 100\% = \textbf{18.29\%}$$

Explanation

The write-down structure compares a certain kind of depreciation (here: goodwill amortization) to total write-downs. Structural ratios can also be broken down to business units or subsidiaries, if available for external use. These ratios help to better understand the composition of a specific expense or source of income (e.g., sales) and allows a detailed analysis of a company. The high amount of goodwill amortization in the example above may be an indicator of the company having paid too much for recent acquisitions, or that in comparison to this figure, the other fixed assets are written-off to a large degree. In the case of goodwill amortization different accounting standards should also be taken into account.

Advantages	Disadvantages
• Allows detailed analysis	• Can fluctuate strongly over time
• Subsidence slopes of companies can be recognized	• Only meaningful in connection to key balance sheet indicators (e.g., fixed assets)

2.13 Personnel expense to total operating expense

Formula

$$\frac{\text{Personnnel expense}}{\text{Total operating expense}} \times 100\%$$

Sample calculation

$$\frac{2,453}{5,004 + 7,857} \times 100\% = \textbf{19.07\%}$$

Explanation

The ratio of personnel expense to total operating expense offers information on the economy of labor. Personnel expense include wages and salaries, social security contributions and contributions for pensions and support. This ratio can be used to review how economically labor is being employed over time. The lower the indicator, the more profitably staff are being employed or are being replaced – which would be reflected by an increase in capital expenditure.

An deterioration (= increase) in this indicator does not necessarily point towards incorrect management decisions, but may also be due to increases in the union agreements or rising social security contributions.

Advantages	Disadvantages
• High practical relevance	• Highly industry-dependent, e.g., due to union agreements
• Recognition of rationalization potential	• Nationwide wage differences make comparison difficult
• Good indicator of labor productivity	• Low meaningfulness if orders fluctuate ("static fixed costs")

2.14 Personnel productivity

Formula

$$\frac{\text{Sales}}{\text{Personnel expense}}$$

Sample calculation

$$\frac{14,019}{2,453} = \textbf{5.72}$$

Explanation

This ratio compares total sales to personnel costs and expresses how much revenue was generated per one Euro of personnel expense (in this case 5.72 EUR). Over time this ratio can be used as an indicator for changes in productivity of a company. When this ratio is higher than the industry-average, this may indicate an efficient use of human resources or an increased intensity of machinery.

The ratio itself is not meaningful enough, instead ratios such as material costs to total costs as well as sales margins should also be considered. The reciprocal of this ratio (Personnel expense/sales x 100%) shows what percentage of sales was booked as personnel expense and thus facilitates company comparisons.

Advantages	Disadvantages
• Personnel's productivity can be analyzed over time	• Personnel costs may be skewed by changes in contributions to social security or union agreements
• Cost saving potential can be revealed	
• Personnel expenses are harder to influence than e.g., marketing expenses	• Only meaningful in connection to other operating expenses and margins

2.15 Sales per employee

Formula

$$\frac{\text{Sales}}{\text{Full-time employees}}$$

Sample calculation

$$\frac{14{,}019 \text{ mn}}{46{,}000} = \textbf{304{,}760}$$

Explanation

The sales per employee ratio provides information on a company's efficiency and provides an indication of how expensive a company is run. By dividing a company's annual sales by the average number of full-time employees, the analyst gets an insight into overhead costs and in turn into possible future profits, as higher sales per employee ratios within the same industry may suggest above average profits. As job cuts can strongly influence this ratio, it should be closely watched over several years in order to identify trends. A continuously rising sales per employee ratio may suggest more streamlined organizations, well-planned capital investments leading to improved efficiency or new products which sell faster than those of the competition.

Advantages	Disadvantages
• Company's efficiency can be analyzed over time	• Not meaningful for cross-industry comparisons
• Indicator for a company's overhead costs and thus for estimating future profits	• Indicator should always be considered in connection with profit margins
• Ratio provides quick sense on a company's situation within the peer group	

Chapter 3

Balance sheet ratios

3.1　Hidden assets

Formula	Sample calculation
Market capitalization – Total equity	12,390 (5,493)
	= 6,897

(Also see market capitalization, page 117)

Explanation

Hidden assets are the portion of equity not disclosed on the balance sheet. Result: Profits or equity appear lower than they really are on the balance sheet date. Hidden assets may occur as a result of:

- Undervaluation or non-capitalization of assets which can be capitalized or
- Waiver or prohibition of possible write-ups or
- Overvaluation of liabilities.

Hidden assets occur either a) compulsorily, b) by using options, c) due to errors in estimates or d) they are intentionally formed. Reversing hidden assets generally leads to higher profits being disclosed.

Advantages	Disadvantages
• Defers taxation, as establishing hidden assets lowers disclosed profits	• Cannot be used directly (market price has to be achieved)
• May offer additional latitude for financing	• For external parties hard or very difficult to calculate if market prices are not known
• The possibility of forming hidden assets offers security	• Hidden assets make it more difficult to calculate yield indicators, which, for example, are based on the capital employed

3.2 Net debt

Formula

Sample calculation

Interest-bearing liabilities	288 + 468
− Cash and cash equivalents	(2,526)
− Short-term investments	0
= Net debt	**= (1,770)**

Explanation

Net debt is interest-bearing debt less liquid funds. As an alternative, it can also be calculated by taking the entire on-balance sheet debt less liquid funds and less pension provisions (these are often equity-like).

Net debt shows the amount of a company's debt, if all liabilities were to be repaid using liquid funds. For example, if a company's liquid funds are greater than its actual debt, then the company is, in fact, debt-free and it exploits the positive effects on its return on equity via the leverage effect (see sample calculation above). However, we must bear in mind that a high level of cash in turn brings a low return and is thus not reasonable from the investor's perspective. In order to be able to properly interpret net debt, this figure should be considered in connection with the cash flow ("dynamic gearing").

Advantages	Disadvantages
• Taking liquid assets into account allows risk to be considered more precisely	• Leasing contracts (e.g., operating leases) should also be considered to ensure comparability
• This is a meaningful early-warning signal for financing risks, in particular if the cash flow is considered	• Little meaning as an absolute figure
	• Maturities are not taken into account

3.3 Goodwill

Formula

> Derivative goodwill = Purchase price − Net asset value
>
> Net asset value = Σ Total assets − (Total liabilities)

Sample calculation

In order to provide an accurate sample calculation, we would have to show an entire acquisition here. We have not done so for reasons of simplicity.

Explanation

Goodwill is the amount in excess of the value of all tangible and intangible assets less debt which a buyer is prepared to pay for an interest while taking into account future income. Goodwill may only be capitalized in the tax accounts and financial accounts if it was actually acquired as part of a corporate acquisition (derivative). Internally generated (original) goodwill may not be carried. Goodwill must be shown separately under intangible assets. Under IFRS and US-GAAP goodwill is no longer amortized in the financial accounts, but is reviewed for impairment and adjusted for such if permanent impairment is ascertained.

Advantages	Disadvantages
• Part of invested capital • Conclusions about the company's "quality" can be drawn in connection with the company's total assets	• Some national accounting laws, such as German GAAP, allow goodwill to be offset against equity. This can lead to distortions

3.4   Average stock

Formula

$$\frac{\text{Opening stock} + \text{Closing stock}}{2}$$

Sample calculation

$$\frac{2,016 + 2,031}{2} = \mathbf{2,023.5}$$

(see balance sheet item: Inventories)

Explanation

Average stock represents the arithmetic average of key stock levels during the fiscal year. It is calculated in particular for goods and materials as well as for receivables and liabilities. The average stock is, for example, a key figure for determining capital requirements, turnover frequency and turnover duration.

Advantages	Disadvantages
• Exceptional deviations during course of year are smoothed out	• Incorrect result if opening and final stock deviate strongly from annual average
• Allows more precise depiction of relationship figures, such as so-called efficiency indicators (e.g., sales to average inventories)	• Depends on inventory size and thus closing date
	• Depends on balance sheet date selected (e.g., if fiscal year is delayed)

3.5   Invested capital

Formula	Sample calculation
Total equity	5,493
+ Non-current provisions	1,140
+ Interest-bearing debt	288 + 468
= Invested capital	**= 7,389**

Explanation

The invested capital is the company's actual capital which bears interest and
which incurs costs, and which is thus the capital which serves the company's
original purpose. This makes it the critical figure to be contrasted against
profits in order to calculate the return. In order to do business successfully,
a company must at least generate the costs of capital for interest-bearing
capital (see also EVA). When calculating the invested capital, as a rule
the cash values of future off-balance sheet activities must be included, as
investors also expect a return from these investments (not applicable in the
example above). These mainly include capitalized leasing expenses.

Advantages	Disadvantages
• Used as a basis for calculating the profitability generated by operating activities • More pertinent in economic terms than pure book values as a result of adjustments	• There are a large number of possible adjustments • Analytical latitude

3.6   Provisions to total capital

Formula

$$\frac{\text{Provisions}}{\text{Total capital}} \times 100\%$$

Sample calculation

$$\frac{1,140}{10,134} \times 100\% = \textbf{11.25\%}$$

Explanation

The ratio provisions to total capital indicates to which degree a company finances itself through provision equivalents. Provisions – although they are financially clearly defined as liabilities – may have equity character when they are structured on a long term basis (e.g., pension provisions).

Financing by pension equivalents is possible by immediately registering the expense for making provisions in the income statement, which has a negative impact on net income. The actual payment is postponed until future fiscal years (deferred payment), respectively, when accruals are reversed it positively affects profits. In the meantime, this amount is available for the production process.

Advantages	Disadvantages
• Pension provisions are not clearly defined as debt and do not lead to constant interest payments	• Can vary significantly over time without obvious reason for external analysts (e.g., provisions for employee's vacation)
• Delivers in the overall context information on the capital structure	• Little significance if more than pension provisions are included, as the timeframe of disposal is not clear (short-term provisions do not serve for financing purposes)

3.7   Reserves to total capital

Formula

$$\frac{\text{Capital reserves + Retained earnings}}{\text{Total capital}} \times 100\%$$

Sample calculation

$$\frac{141 + 3,789}{10,134} \times 100\% = \textbf{38.78\%}$$

Explanation

This ratio describes the percentage of capital reserves and retained earnings in comparison to total capital. Reserves are part of the shareholders' equity and consist of capital reserves (derived from additional capital raised externally, e.g., capital surplus at IPO) and retained earnings (i.e., derived from past income). From a creditors point of view, a high degree of reserves offers security for existing and additional loans. Thus, the higher the percentage of reserves to total capital, the lower the risk of non-performing loans for the lender. Over time the external analyst is able to tell whether the ratio, and thus the company's capital base, increases or decreases. A decrease may eventually lead to a total loss of shareholders' equity (including capital stock) and thus endanger a company's existence.

Advantages	Disadvantages
• Helps to assess collateral levels	• Reserves which are not stated in the balance sheet (hidden assets) are not considered
• Indicator for self-financing tendencies of a company	
	• Only significant in connection to the length of the company's existence
• The higher the amount of equity, the higher the amount of liable assets	
	• Capital reserves may vary strongly over time in US-GAAP accounting due to fluctuations in exchange rates

3.8   Inventories to total capital

Formula

$$\frac{\text{Inventories}}{\text{Total assets or capital}} \times 100\%$$

Sample calculation

$$\frac{2,016}{10,134} \times 100\% = \mathbf{19.89\%}$$

Explanation

The ratio of inventories to total assets or capital delivers an insight into a company's asset distribution. It should always be compared to the industry's benchmark (e.g., the ratio in the manufacturing industry is of course in general larger than in the service sector). An increasing ratio over time at constant revenues may thus be an indication for sales difficulties.

An objective for many companies (especially in the automobile industry) has been to keep inventory costs sustainably low, which can be achieved through just-in-time production. From an external point of view, the ratio provides some information with respect to the time needed for liquidating assets.

Advantages	Disadvantages
• Usually industry-specific comparable ratios are available • Over time a first indicator for basic structural changes	• Valuation of inventories depends heavily on balance sheet policy (IFRS / US-GAAP / German GAAP) • No reference to income statement (e.g., store house expenses), thus little significance • Differentiation between raw materials, semi-finished and finished goods necessary for detailed analysis

3.9 Degree of asset depreciation

Formula

$$\frac{\text{Accumulated depreciation on property, plant and equipment}}{\text{Historical cost of property, plant and equipment}}$$

Sample calculation

$$\frac{2{,}650 + 402}{2{,}736 + 2{,}650 + 402} = 0.53$$

Explanation

The degree of asset depreciation is not stated in years, but rather as a number between zero and one. Zero indicates that all assets have recently been acquired and have not depreciated, whereas one means that all assets have been completely written off.

A value of close to one may indicate an out-dated production technology (= competitive disadvantage) which may result in a below-average productivity in comparison to the industry. Of course this ratio should always be considered in conjunction with the specific industry's technological state of the art. In addition, one should consider that the degree of asset depreciation depends heavily on the company's write-down policy. For example, assets are often written-off as fast as possible, although economic use takes place years beyond the write-off period.

Advantages	Disadvantages
• Important figure for manufacturing companies • Indicator for investment cycles and needs	• Comparison is distorted if asset retirement posting are not made (residual book value) • Little significance for service companies • May lead to distortion if different write-down methods are applied • Asset structure can be influenced (purchase vs. leasing)

Chapter 4

Cash flow ratios

4.1 Cash flow from operating activities

Formula	Sample calculation
EBIT	1,452
− Taxes	(711)
+ Depreciation and amortization	492
± Change in long-term provisions (excl. interest)	(33)
± Profit (loss) on disposal of fixed assets	3
± Change in working capital	45
= **Cash flow from operating activities**	= **1,248**

Explanation

Cash flow from operating activities indicates the cash flow which stems from operating activities during the period under review. The cash flow thus, to a certain extent, shows the financial result from operations. This is shown by adjusting EBIT, alternatively net income by the amounts which did not lead to the cash flow or that cannot be allocated to operating activities. The cash flow plays a major role in corporate valuations in particular, as the total forecast (free) cash flows are discounted to the their present value (e.g., Discounted cash flow method).

Advantages	Disadvantages
• Provides information on "available funds"	• Hardly possible to compare companies
• Cannot be manipulated as easily as net income	• Cash flow itself does not indicate if a company was able to gene-rate shareholder value
• Good retrospective indicator for a company's success	
• Calculation shows the extent to which write-downs affect earnings ("write-downs have to be earned")	

4.2 Cash flow from investing activities

Formula	Sample calculation
Capital expenditures, net (Capex)	(474)
+ Financial expenditures, net (Finex)	0
± Other investing cash flow items, total	150
= Cash flow from investing activities	**= (324)**

Explanation

Cash flow from investing activities shows the balance of cash funds that the company has invested in financial assets and property, plant and equipment or obtained from the sale of these assets.

As a rule, the cash flow from investing activities should be negative, because it shows that the company has reinvested the funds it has earned in the company's continued existence or growth. The cash flow from investments in fixed assets is often also referred to as "Capex" (capital expenditure), the cash flow from investments in financial assets as "Finex" (financial expenditure).

Advantages	Disadvantages
• Provides information on how funds are used	• No information on whether investments are made for maintenance or expansion
• In conjunction with cash flow from operating activities, the ratio provides information on additional financing volume needed	• Varies strongly over time
	• No information on how sensible an investment is

4.3 Cash flow from financing activities

Formula	Sample calculation
Issuance of stock, net	0
− Total cash dividends paid	(354)
+ Issuance of debt (bonds and credits)	0
− Payments for redemption of bonds and credits	0
− Interest payments and other financing cash flow items	(141)
= Cash flow from financing activities	**= (495)**

Explanation

Cash flow from financing activities offers information on the balance of cash inflows and outflows from financing activities. Inflows may result from new equity (e.g., from going public or a secondary placement for a capital increase on the stock market) or from increasing debt (e.g., from issuing a bond or taking out a loan), outflows stem from disbursements to shareholders or repaying liabilities.

Advantages	Disadvantages
• Shows the origin of additional funding	• Not meaningful when taken alone
• Provides readers with key information on the company's financing activities and abilities	• Varies strongly over time
• Combining the cash flow from operating activities, the cash flow from investing activities and the cash flow from financing activities allows the change in cash and cash equivalents to be calculated	• Only allows limited conclusions regarding future performance to be drawn

4.4 Free cash flow

Formula	Sample calculation
Cash flow from operating activities	1,248
− Capex, net	(474)
= Free cash flow	**= 774**

Explanation

The free cash flow refers to the free funds available to the company. These funds describe the company's potential value for investors and creditors and are available for reinvestment of profits, or the payment of interest or credit redemption. The future free cash flows are generally the starting point for company valuation.

Advantages	Disadvantages
• Can be used as a basis for ascertaining a company's value	• The amount of debt and equity costs must be calculated separately
• Does not depend on the form of financing	• Can be subject to strong fluctuations, for example from investment cycles
• Can be calculated from the financial statements	

4.5 Cash flow

Formula   **Sample calculation**

Net income	882
+ Depreciation and amortization	492
± Change in long-term provisions	(51)
= Cash flow	**= 1,323**

Explanation

The alternative approach in comparison to operating cash flow for calculating cash flow is to add depreciation and amortization as well as changes in long-term provisions to net income. As depreciation does not lead to a direct cash outflow it does not affect a company's liquid funds and is therefore added to net income. Cash flow is a better indicator than net income, as different write-off methods are eliminated, making cross-company comparisons easier. One has to bear in mind though that different cash flow definitions exist, e.g. changes in working capital are also considered for calculating a company's cash flow.

Advantages	Disadvantages
• Cash flow less manipulated than net income	• Different definitions of cash flow exist, which limits comparability
• Intuitive	• Can be subject to strong fluctuations depending on investment cycles
• Easy to calculate	• Cross-industry comparisons are hardly possible

4.6 Capex to depreciation and amortization

Formula

$$\frac{\text{Capex, net}}{\text{Depreciation and amortization}} \times 100\%$$

Sample calculation

$$\frac{474}{492} \times 100\% = \textbf{96.34\%}$$

Explanation

This indicator compares net cash flow from investments in fixed assed (or capital expenditure = Capex) to depreciation and amortization for the period. Our sample calculation shows, that new investments were slightly lower than depreciation. Depreciation was thus nearly fully reinvested, which allows us to conclude that the company invests in order to keep operations stable. A ratio higher than 100% would indicate further expansion. This indicators' greatest added value is that the observer has a figure they can use to gain a feeling for the amount of new investments.

Advantages	Disadvantages
• Allows the amount of investments in expansion to be calculated	• Ratio depends on write-down method
• Conclusions can be drawn about maintenance investments	• Capex may not be confused with Finex (financial expenditure)
	• Only a meaningful figure when observed over time

4.7   Capex to sales

Formula

$$\frac{\text{Capex, net}}{\text{Sales}} \times 100\%$$

Sample calculation

$$\frac{474}{14,019} \times 100\% = \mathbf{3.38\%}$$

Explanation

The indicator Capex to sales is the ratio of net annual investments in a company's assets as a component of the cash flow from investing activities to total sales.

This indicator thus expresses the percentage of revenue that was re-invested. This indicator is dynamic and thus more difficult to impact than static indicators.

Advantages	Disadvantages
• Allows increases in efficiency to be calculated	• No clear information, as a lower ratio could express both efficiency increases as well as omissions in investment policy
• Allows conclusions to be drawn regarding omissions in investment policy	
	• Only a meaningful figure when taken over time
• Revenue is less susceptible to accounting policy (and is thus a "purer" indicator than depreciation/amortization)	• Can fluctuate heavily over time

Chapter 5

Profitability ratios

5.1 EBIT margin

Formula

$$\frac{EBIT}{Sales} \times 100\%$$

Sample calculation

$$\frac{1,452}{14,019} \times 100\% = \textbf{10.36\%}$$

Explanation

The EBIT margin (or operating margin) shows the percentage of earnings from operations before interest, taxes and the financial result that a company was able to record per unit of revenue. This indicator thus provides information on a company's earnings power. The higher the EBIT margin, the stronger the impact of a change in sales will be on earnings. If no positive EBIT margins are generated over a longer period, then in the case of established companies, the business model must be questioned. The EBIT margin is suitable for use as a relative indicator in international, cross-industry comparisons of companies. When considered over time, this indicator provides information on whether a company has been able to increase its earnings power. If the company has not been able to succeed in this endeavor, then the reasons for this should be analyzed.

Advantages	Disadvantages
• Simplifies international comparability	• Various write-down methods make comparability more difficult
• Independent of national tax requirements	• Distortion from inclusion of income which cannot be directly allocated to operating activities
• Independent of type of financing	
• Used for comparison over time	• The quality of operating results can worsen even though the earnings themselves are rising (e.g., if R&D costs fall)

5.2   EBITDA margin

Formula

$$\frac{\text{EBITDA}}{\text{Sales}} \times 100\%$$

Sample calculation

$$\frac{1,944}{14,019} \times 100\% = \textbf{13.87\%}$$

Explanation

The EBITDA margin taxes show the percentage of operating income before interest expense (income), and depreciation/amortization that a company was able to record per unit of revenue.

This indicator thus provides information on a company's earnings strength. The EBITDA margin is a valuable indicator in particular in international comparisons, as the various accounting standards, tax laws and write-down policies do not impact calculation of the margin. In addition, this indicator is also suitable for use by young companies which are not yet recording any profits. In these cases, a positive EBITDA margin indicates the ability of the business model to work profitably.

Advantages	Disadvantages
• Simplifies international comparisons	• Strategic equity interests are not considered if not consolidated
• Not impacted by various write-down modalities	• Significant cost blocks can be eliminated from the income statement via the formation of joint ventures
• Allows statements to be made on expense development over time	• Varying expense components can impact the amount and quality of this indicator

5.3 Gross profit margin

Formula

$$\frac{\text{Gross profit}}{\text{Sales}} \times 100\%$$

Sample calculation

$$\frac{9,015}{14,019} \times 100\% = \mathbf{64.31\%}$$

Explanation

The gross profit margin tells us the percentage of sales that the company has available as gross profit (total sales less cost of sales). Retailers also speak of the retail margin. The growth of this indicator shows how a company's procurement prices have changed. The indicator also offers information on the possible latitude available for price cuts if competition becomes more intense.

Advantages	Disadvantages
• The gross profit margin allows conclusions to be drawn about production and procurement efficiency	• The gross profit margin is only meaningful in conjunction with the EBIT margin, as there may be changes to accounting policy due to the different classification of production costs
• Used in industry comparisons	
• Provides information on a company's competitive strength (possibility to cut prices)	• Not meaningful in cross-industry comparisons

5.4 Return on total capital

Formula

$$\frac{\text{Net income} + \text{Income tax} + \text{Interest expense, net operating}}{\text{Total liabilities and shareholders' equity}} \times 100\%$$

Sample calculation

$$\frac{882 + 594 + 12}{10,134} \times 100\% = \textbf{14.68\%}$$

Explanation

This ratio shows the interest on total capital, which comprises both total equity and liabilities. In this ratio, taxes and interest expense are added to net income in order to achieve better comparability. Over time, observers can interpret the company's performance and make comparisons with other companies. This indicator is generally used as a starting point for all further analyses using profitability indicators.

Advantages	Disadvantages
• Very meaningful regarding return on total capital	• Highly dependent on accounting policy
• Cross-industry comparisons possible	• Poor meaningfulness for high-growth companies

5.5　Return on equity

Formula

$$\frac{\text{Net income excl. extraordinary items}}{\text{Total equity}} \times 100\%$$

Sample calculation

$$\frac{882}{5,493} \times 100\% = \textbf{16.06\%}$$

Explanation

The return on equity is calculated by dividing net income excluding extraordinary items by total equity, i.e. the common shareholders' equity. This indicator shows the rate of return on shareholders' capital for the period. Given constant profits, the return on equity increases the lower the level of equity employed (leverage effect).

A company's goal must be to generate a return that corresponds to the interest rate on the capital markets plus an industry-dependent risk premium (in total generally between 5–10%).

Advantages	Disadvantages
• Highly relevant in practice	• Returns should be observed over the long term
• Good indicator for investments	• Debt is not taken into account
• Meaningful in cross-industry comparisons	• Accounting options can falsify net income

5.6 Return on average total assets

Formula

$$\frac{\text{Net income}}{\text{Average total assets}} \times 100\%$$

Sample calculation

$$\frac{882}{\dfrac{(10{,}134 + 9{,}894)}{2}} \times 100\% = \mathbf{8.81\%}$$

Explanation

This ratio compares net income to average total assets, which corresponds to the return on total capital. In this ratio, taxes and interest expense are not adjusted, which makes comparability between companies more difficult, as net income is strongly affected by accounting policies. Over time, analysts can interpret the company's performance.

Advantages	Disadvantages
• Good indicator over time for evaluating a company's performance in the long-term	• Cross-company comparisons are difficult
• Easy to calculate	• Depreciation policy has a major impact on net income and assets
• Average total assets makes indicator less static	• Companies that do not invest are for years are rewarded with an increasing return on average total assets
	• Leasing is not included

5.7 Return on invested capital (ROIC)

Formula

$$\frac{\text{NOPAT}}{\text{Invested capital}} \times 100\%$$

Sample calculation

$$\frac{851}{7,389} \times 100\% = \textbf{11.52\%}$$

Explanation

Return on invested capital (ROIC) shows the return on the company's adjusted, invested capital. In order to take various financing structures into account, when calculating this indicator the invested capital (calculation see page 43) is compared with NOPAT (see page 26). At the same time, ROIC is also the preliminary stage in calculating economic value added (see page 133), which tells us that a company only creates value for its shareholders (so-called shareholder value) if the ROIC is higher than a company's cost of capital.

Advantages	Disadvantages
• Used in calculating the profitability generated purely from operating activities	• Adjustments allow a certain latitude
• Invested capital reflects the pure operating assets	• Costs of capital are not taken into account
• Components are also taken into account that are not reflected in total assets, such as leasing	• We must not forget, that assets which are not considered as operating assets must also generate a return

5.8 Return on capital employed (ROCE)

Formula

$$\frac{\text{EBIT}}{\text{Fixed assets, net} + \text{Working capital}} \times 100\%$$

Sample calculation

$$\frac{1,452}{3,093 + 3,453} \times 100\% = \textbf{22.18\%}$$

Explanation

Return on capital employed (ROCE) contrasts EBIT with the capital employed during a period, which allows us to calculate the company's earnings power. As a rule, capital employed is defined as being an asset, on the liabilities side it would correspond to equity plus pension provisions and net financial liabilities.

The problem with ROCE is that the indicator is based on residual book values (that have already been written down). This means that the returns would always increase over time, even if the company made no further investments.

Advantages	Disadvantages
• Measures pure operational success	• Based on accounting material
• An adjustment is made to income and assets which do not serve the operating process	• Costs of capital are not taken into account
• The return is shown as a ratio on capital employed (significantly better indicator than income after tax)	

5.9 Return on investment (ROI)

Formula

Return on sales × Turnover (or capital turnover)

$$= \frac{\text{Net income}}{\text{Sales}} \times \frac{\text{Sales}}{\text{Total liabilities and shareholders' equity}} \times 100\%$$

Sample calculation

$$\frac{882}{14{,}019} \times \frac{14{,}019}{10{,}134} \times 100\% = 0.063 \times 1.38 \times 100\% = \textbf{8.69\%}$$

Explanation

Return on investment comprises the return on sales multiplied with the turnover of total equity and liabilities. If summarized (cancel out sales from the fractions) this would only show the profit on total equity and liabilities. However the expanded formula shows the value driver of return on investment in a more transparent manner. When taken over time, this indicator helps in measuring the performance of the capital employed and the expanded formula allows the reasons for changes to be recognized more quickly.

Advantages	Disadvantages
• Key indicator for investment decisions	• Investment activities can negatively impact this indicator
• Comparable across industries	• Write-downs for assets have a major impact
• Transparency for factors that cause change over time (costs, price, margins)	• Companies that do not invest are rewarded with a better ROI

5.10   Return on sales

Formula

$$\frac{\text{Net income}}{\text{Sales}} \times 100\%$$

Sample calculation

$$\frac{882}{14{,}019} \times 100\% = \mathbf{6.3\%}$$

Explanation

If we divide profits (net income) by sales we can see the return on sales. This indicator shows the percentage of sales accrues to the company as profits after the deduction of all costs, the financial result, taxes and extraordinary items. The return on sales is a meaningful figure, in particular within a company when comparing individual group units, to assess which unit was able to generate which return. This allows a differentiation to be made between profitable and non-profitable business units. However, profits are highly subject to fluctuations, which means that the EBIT margin is more meaningful than the return on sales.

Advantages	Disadvantages
• Information on productivity • May be possible to recognize cost-cutting potential	• Highly product-dependent, thus limited comparability • Very highly industry-dependent • No information whether extra-ordinary factors improved the ratio or not • Profits can be manipulated more easily than cash flow

5.11 Cash flow margin

Formula

$$\frac{\text{Cash flow from operating activities}}{\text{Sales}} \times 100\%$$

Sample calculation

$$\frac{1,248}{14,019} \times 100\% = \textbf{8.90\%}$$

Explanation

The cash flow margin, also known as cash flow profitability is calculated by comparing the cash flow from operating activities to sales of a fiscal year. The cash flow margin is therefore an indicator, what percentage of total sales is available for investments, credit redemption or dividend payments. It is also meaningful for assessing the company's earnings and financing power, as cash flow is less manipulated than EBIT for example. As a consequence, a decreasing EBIT margin over time due to increased depreciation and amortization can be put into perspective when comparing it to the cash flow margin.

Advantages	Disadvantages
• Hard to manipulate for purposes of balance sheet policies	• Can vary strongly over time
• Good indicator for operative earnings power of a company over time	• The cash flow of a single period has only minimal significance

5.12 Reinvestment rate (I)

Formula

$$\frac{\Delta \text{ Invested capital}}{\text{NOPAT}} \times 100\%$$

Sample calculation

$$\frac{7{,}389 - 7{,}104}{851} \times 100\% = \mathbf{33.49\%}$$

Explanation

The reinvestment rate shows the proportion of the operating result after taxes (NOPAT, for calculation see page 26) is reinvested in new assets which will be used to generate income in subsequent years (for calculation of invested capital see page 43). In the example above, the reinvestment rate is positive, as the invested capital increased. In case NOPAT remains at this level in future years, the return on invested capital (ROIC, see page 67) would slightly decrease.

Advantages	Disadvantages
• Information on financial strength (NOPAT is a good approximation for cash flow) • Information on innovational strength and readiness • Intention to increase productivity can be recognized	• Highly industry-dependent • Poor information given changes in production

5.13 Working capital to sales

Formula

$$\frac{\text{Working capital}}{\text{Sales}} \times 100\%$$

Sample calculation

$$\frac{3,453}{14,019} \times 100\% = \textbf{24.63\%}$$

Explanation

This indicator shows the ratio of working capital (see page 92) to sales and thus provides external observers the turnover of working capital for generating revenues. The ratio is strongly industry dependent, as retailers with very high turnover ratios need far less working capital for generating sales than mechanical engineering or automobile companies.

In the example above, there is a large amount of working capital at almost 25% of revenues. If we now consider another ratio, for example current assets/current liabilities ((6,888/2,814) x 100% = 244.78%), we can see that the company has more than twice as much current funding as would be necessary to repay the current liabilities. In this case, the high liquidity would initially make a very positive impression, however at the expense of profitability.

Advantages	Disadvantages
• Shows a company's capital lock-up	• Cross-industry comparisons are not meaningful
• Additional investment requirements can be calculated in particular for capacity expansions	• Capacity expansions (changes) can dilute the indicator's meaningfulness
• Allows conclusions to be drawn on the efficiency of the production process when compared within the industry	

5.14 Sales to inventory

Formula

$$\frac{\text{Sales}}{\text{Average total inventories}}$$

Sample calculation

$$\frac{14,019}{2,023.5} = \mathbf{6.93}$$

Explanation

This ratio shows the relationship between a company's revenues and its inventories. If this ratio rises over time, this should generally be regarded as being positive, as less capital is locked-up in the form of inventories. The company's goal must be to keep its inventories as low as possible without delaying deliveries. This is primarily due to the fact that the locked-up capital does not bring any return, but rather has a negative impact on returns as a result of losses or higher warehousing costs. The ratio should be compared to the industry average, i.e. retailers oftentimes only sell the supplier's products on consignment. This has the effect for the supplier, that although the products have been distributed they are still booked as inventories as long as the retailer has not sold them to the customer.

Advantages	Disadvantages
• Allows capacity requirements to be estimated	• Observed on two specific dates
• Information on financing requirements	• Highly industry-dependent
• Recognizable optimization potential	• Changes in the ratio can not be clearly identified due to one-time effects (specific date) or goods on consignment (retail power)

5.15 Property, plant and equipment to sales

Formula

$$\frac{\text{Property, plant and equipment}}{\text{Sales}} \times 100\%$$

Sample calculation

$$\frac{2{,}736}{14{,}019} \times 100\% = \mathbf{19.52\%}$$

Explanation

This ratio compares the value of the deployed tangible assets (at actual book values) to the sales thereby generated and shows the production process's asset intensity of a company.

Usually this ratio should be viewed in connection to the reinvestment rate (see page 99) and net investments (important figure for asset intense companies). Moreover, the external analyst receives a better insight when comparing the ratio to past figures or industry standards, if the useful life of assets (i.e. the period until replacement) is considered.

Advantages	Disadvantages
• Serves to determine production efficiency over time	• Only meaningful in connection with accumulated depreciation and reinvestment rate
• Helpful for manufacturing companies	
	• A large portfolio of land and buildings may skew the resulting ratio
• Provides clarity of necessary expansion investments if future sales figures are given	
	• No consideration of leasing

5.16 Fixed asset turnover

Formula

$$\frac{\text{Depreciation on property, plant and equipment}}{\text{Averaged property, plant and equipment at historical costs}}$$

Sample calculation

$$\frac{402}{\dfrac{(2{,}736 + 2{,}650) + (2{,}751 + 2{,}248)}{2}} = \frac{402}{5{,}192.5} = \mathbf{0.08}$$

Explanation

This indicator shows the proportion of fixed assets which were "earned" again in this period. This figure shows us that fixed assets at historical cost were turned over at a rate of 0.08 times. An increase in the factor means that the period of use of the assets is shorter, however this figure is easily distorted as a result of write-down methods for various groups/investment focuses. Expressed in years, at an asset turnover of 0.08 it would take 12.5 years before the write-downs had covered the book value of fixed assets.

Advantages	Disadvantages
• Good industry comparison	• Depends on write-down methods
• Meaningful for technical innovations	• No information on productivity and useful lives
• High transparency regarding investment activities	• Low meaningfulness as a result of non-transparent investment focuses

5.17 Current asset turnover

Formula

$$\frac{\text{Sales}}{\text{Average current assets}}$$

Sample calculation

$$\frac{14{,}019}{\dfrac{(6{,}888 + 6{,}552)}{2}} = \mathbf{2.09}$$

Explanation

The current asset turnover shows how often a unit of current assets was turned over in the period under review. For this purpose, the average stock of current assets corresponds to the arithmetic average of the starting and closing stock of current assets.

The turnover shows the lock-up period for the current assets and allows conclusions to be drawn about the amount of capital required. The higher this indicator, the more positive. Too low a turnover has the consequence of reducing the warehouse stocks (e.g., via just in time), the cash in hand (e.g., via reinvestment) or the reduction of receivables (e.g., factoring). Among retailers, turnover is the key indicator for managing merchandise.

We can also express current asset turnover in terms of days: 365/2.09 = 174.64 days. That means, that it takes approx. six months to turn over the entire current assets.

Advantages	Disadvantages
• Used for comparisons within an industry	• Hard to compare across industries
• Provides information on the efficiency of the sales process (e.g., for retail companies)	• The more differentiated a company's activities, the lower the meaningfulness
• More important than the total asset turnover for retail companies	• Only meaningful for comparable products

5.18 Total asset turnover

Formula

$$\frac{\text{Sales}}{\text{Total assets}}$$

Sample calculation

$$\frac{14,019}{10,134} = \textbf{1.38}$$

Explanation

The total asset turnover shows how often all assets (and thus also the total shareholders' equity and liabilities) were turned over during the period under review, i.e., the extent to which the assets held are actually turned over in terms of sales.

This turnover ratio can also be expressed in days: 365/1.38 = 264.5 days. This means that it takes approx. nine months to earn the amount of total assets.

Advantages	Disadvantages
• Information on duration of capital lock-up	• Highly industry dependent
• Information on capacity requirements	• No information on profitability
• Good information on turnover period	

5.19   Receivables turnover

Formula

$$\frac{\text{Sales}}{\text{Average total receivables}}$$

Sample calculation

$$\frac{14,019}{\dfrac{(2,064 + 2,025)}{2}} = \textbf{6.86}$$

Explanation

Receivables turnover shows the factor by which sales exceed the company's average total receivables. The lower this indicator, the greater the danger for the company that, if a customer becomes unable to make payment, the company itself will run into liquidity problems. When analyzing this indicator, we must also consider the number of debtors over which the receivables are distributed on average.

If there are only a few debtors, then the dependency on the debtors' solvency and payment readiness increases. The greater the receivables turnover, the faster the respective company's receivables are paid. If the receivables turnover is too low, this can generally be optimized by active credit control. As a result, this indicator also reflects the company's ability to collect outstanding receivables. The counterpart of receivables turnover is days sales outstanding (DSO), please see the following page.

Advantages	Disadvantages
• Information on liquidity	• Possible distortion from a few, very old receivables
• Information on debtors' credit-worthiness	• No information on number of customers (risk distribution)
• Information on need for financing	• No information on average size of outstanding payments
• Information on company's credit control	• Cross-industry comparisons are difficult

5.20 Days sales outstanding (DSO)

Formula

$$\frac{\text{Average trade receivables}}{\text{Sales}} \times 365$$

Sample calculation

$$\frac{\dfrac{(2{,}064 + 2{,}025)}{2}}{14{,}019} \times 365 = \textbf{53.23}$$

Explanation

DSO shows the average number of days it takes for a receivable to be paid (customer target). The ratio is also known as average collection period. The longer this period, the worse for a company, as the debtor is granted a (generally) interest-free loan for this period. The shorter this period, the lower the interest to be borne by the creditor and the smaller the risk of default. Measures to decrease the days sales outstanding include, for example, increasing or granting discounts, improved credit control, converting to direct debits or factoring. An increase in DSO can also be due to large sales being booked just before the end of the year that are only due in the following fiscal year, or customers delaying payment to the upcoming fiscal year.

Advantages	Disadvantages
• Meaningful element when estimating future net current assets	• Highly dependent on customer groups (wholesale – retail)
• Information on capital lock-up/financing intensity	• No information on number of customers (risk distribution)
• Recognition on risk of receivable default	• Difficult to compare across industries
• Over time can be used as an indicator for credit control	

5.21 Days payables outstanding

Formula

$$\frac{\text{Average trade liabilities}}{\text{Cost of sales}} \times 365$$

Sample calculation

$$\frac{\dfrac{(909 + 879)}{2}}{5,004} \times 365 = \mathbf{65.21}$$

Explanation

The ratio days payables outstanding shows the average number of days needed for trade liabilities to be paid by the company (here approx. two months). Alternatively sales are used instead of cost of sales for calculating this ratio. A long turnover period at first improves the company's liquidity. Basically trade liabilities are a non-interest bearing credit by the supplier, which helps to finance the operating business. On the other hand, if a company does not have professional cash management, financing by means of trade payables can become very expensive when the company does not take advantage of discounts. For this reason, a long turnover period may also be an indicator for liquidity problems.

Advantages	Disadvantages
• Indicator for payment targets	• No information on maturities or payment morality
• Indicator of a company's credit worthiness	• Age structure of liabilities is not illustrated
• Information on a company's solvency and paying habits	• Receivables are not considered

5.22 Inventory turnover

Formula

$$\frac{\text{Cost of sales}}{\text{Average total inventories}}$$

Sample calculation

$$\frac{5,004}{\dfrac{(2,016 + 2,031)}{2}} = \textbf{2.47}$$

Explanation

Inventory turnover provides information on the speed at which inventories are sold and provides observers with an indicator which can be used to calculate the company's performance. Taken over time this indicator offers information on the management's efforts and success in increasing inventory turnover. Expressed in days, $365/2.47 = 147.8$ days, it means that the company needs approx. five months to sell the inventories it has bought in.

In order to express the complete operating process in days, i.e., the number of days needed between buying in the inventories until the date on which the receivables are collected, we need the following information: Inventory turnover in days + days sales outstanding (DSO) = $147.8 + 53.2 = 201$ days. This means that the company needs more than half a year for its operating cycle.

Advantages	Disadvantages
• Helpful for analyzing the company's operating activities	• Individual product groups must be observed for diversified companies
• Assessment of the sales process and the warehousing process	• Highly industry-dependent
• Warehousing performance provides information on capital lock-up and costs of capital	

5.23 Payables turnover

Formula

$$\frac{\text{Cost of sales} \times \text{VAT}}{\text{Average trade liabilities}}$$

Sample calculation

$$\frac{5,004 \times 1.2}{\dfrac{(909 + 879)}{2}} = \mathbf{6.72}$$

Explanation

The ratio payables turnover shows the company's payment practices in the period under review. From an investor's perspective, a reduction in this indicator over a specific period can mean that the company's ability to make payment is deteriorating and that it is tending to pay liabilities at an increasingly later date. However, a reduction can also represent a positive development if the company is making increasing use of payment targets and thus making more profitable use of its own liquidity.

Advantages	Disadvantages
• Information on liquidity situation	• Late customer target can either point towards market strength or creditworthiness problems
• Information on creditworthiness	
• Information on the company's payment ability or payment practices	• Highly industry-dependent
	• Late payment target can lead to expensive financing (loss of discounts)

5.24 Capital turnover

Formula

$$\frac{\text{Sales}}{\text{Total equity + Total liabilities}}$$

Sample calculation

$$\frac{14,019}{5,493 + 2,577 + 1,665} = \mathbf{1.44}$$

Explanation

The capital turnover shows total revenue compared to total liabilities and shareholders' equity. The fact that a company turns over its assets quickly generates margins. A company with an equal return on revenues but a lower ratio of sales to total liabilities and shareholders' equity would generate lower profits due to the higher fixed costs and capital lock-up costs. It is also true that the higher this ratio, the lower the amount of capital required (due to the shorter pre-financing period).

Advantages	Disadvantages
• May be used to expand the traditional Du Pont formula (indicator tree to calculate ROI) • Indicates the effectiveness of capital use	• Total capital is not a sufficient indicator to calculate the actual capital employed which serves to generate sales, as, for example, leasing expenses are not taken into account

Chapter 6

Liquidity ratios

6.1 Equity ratio

Formula

$$\frac{\text{Total equity}}{\text{Total capital}} \times 100\%$$

Sample calculation

$$\frac{5,493}{10,134} \times 100\% = \textbf{54.20\%}$$

Explanation

The equity ratio describes the relationship between equity and total capital or total shareholders' equity and liabilities. As a rule, the more equity a company has available the better its credit-worthiness, the higher its financial stability and the more independent the company is from lenders. However, as equity is more expensive than debt (see also WACC, page 131), a high equity ratio depresses the return on capital employed. When calculating the equity ratio, we can either use total capital or, as generally practiced by financial analysts in particular when calculating the costs of capital, only use the sum of total equity and interest-bearing debt.

Advantages	Disadvantages
• Shows the type and composition of capital	• Depends heavily on industry and valuations
• Easy to calculate	• Hidden assets reduce the actual value of equity
• Serves to calculate the debt level (leverage) and allows assumptions to be made about a company's stability	• Balance sheet figures are now often being replaced by frequently used market values (e.g., use of market capitalization instead of balance sheet equity to calculate costs of capital)
• Helpful in same-industry comparisons as an indicator for a company's relative financial strength	

6.2 Total liabilities to total capital (leverage)

Formula

$$\frac{\text{Total liabilities}}{\text{Total capital}} \times 100\%$$

Sample calculation

$$\frac{2,577 + 1,655}{10,134} \times 100\% = \mathbf{41.86\%}$$

Explanation

The leverage describes the ratio of total liabilities to total capital. In the course of company valuations, financial analysts often only use total liabilities as the sum of interest-bearing liabilities plus the capitalized value of future leasing commitments, as these are also interest-bearing.

The ratio of liabilities to total capital allows assumptions to be made about a company's financial stability. The growth of this indicator should always be considered together with the company's assets. If these include hidden liabilities as a result of lower market values, this has a negative impact on the leverage ratio. Over the past few years, this has contributed, for example, to balance sheet recession.

Advantages	Disadvantages
• The amount of the ratio of liabilities to total capital can be viewed as a factor dependent on the company or product life-cycle (as a rule, the older a company, the higher the possible leverage due to increasing creditworthiness) • The quality of the assets can be compared to the leverage (e.g., risk if goodwill is mostly covered by liabilities)	• Depends heavily on industry and valuations • Earlier adjustments (e.g., impairment of goodwill that reduces equity) could lead to distortions • Forms of off-balance sheet financing (e.g., leasing) are generally not taken into account

6.3　Total liabilities to total equity (gearing)

Formula

$$\frac{\text{Total liabilities}}{\text{Total equity}} \times 100\%$$

Sample calculation

$$\frac{2,577 + 1,665}{5,493} \times 100\% = \mathbf{77.23\%}$$

Explanation

This ratio shows the relationship between the company's liabilities and equity financing. Some analysts also call it gearing ratio. As a general rule, the higher the gearing ratio, the more dependent a company is on external creditors. If the leverage effect is considered when assessing a company's gearing ratio, we can see that for profitability reasons a higher gearing ratio can be regarded as being positive under certain conditions as well as. As a result, the gearing ratio should never be considered alone, but always in connection with the company's earnings position.

Advantages	Disadvantages
• A connection between the gearing ratio and the return on equity can be shown in formal terms (the lower the gearing ratio, the more likely it is to be able to take up additional debt to utilize the leverage effect) • A risk profile can be calculated in connection with the maturities of various asset components	• Cross-industry comparisons are difficult to portray • Adjustments to equity resulting from accounting policy can lead to distortions • Forms of off-balance sheet activities (e.g., leasing) are generally not taken into account

6.4 Leverage structure

Formula

$$\frac{\text{Trade liabilities} + \text{Short-term liabilities}}{\text{Total liabilities}} \times 100\%$$

Sample calculation

$$\frac{909 + 468}{2,577 + 1,665} \times 100\% = \mathbf{32.46\%}$$

Explanation

The leverage structure compares short-term liabilities to total liabilities. This ratio therefore expresses what percentage of total liabilities will actually lead to a cash outflow to external creditors on a short-term basis. In general, companies in danger of insolvency show an increased percentage of leverage structure than solvent companies. For an ongoing analysis the maturity and conditions of all liability components should be taken into account. Although trade liabilities are usually non-interest bearing and thus initially positive for a company's financing, they can become the most expensive form of financing when a company does not take advantage of discounts.

Advantages	Disadvantages
• Indicator for possible financial difficulties when the percentage of short-term liabilities is very high	• Disregards costs of asset components
• Indicator for maturities	• Does not consider maturities of financed assets (also see "golden financing rule")
• Indicator for the necessity of liquid funds	• Is not meaningful without considering liquidity ratios

6.5   Dynamic gearing

Formula

$$\frac{\text{Net debt}}{\text{Free cash flow}}$$

Sample calculation

$$\frac{(1,770)}{774} = \textbf{(2.29)}$$

Explanation

This ratio shows how many years a company would need to be able to repay its (net) liabilities from its free cash flow. The ratio is also known as net debt service or duration of debt redemption.

In the manufacturing industry, a factor of up to four is regarded as being excellent – a factor of greater than ten or even a negative cash flow over several periods may lead to the danger of insolvency. In the above example, net debt is negative, as the company is in fact free of debt. Nevertheless one time effects should be analyzed before evaluating this ratio. Moreover, off-balance sheet liabilities, such as leasing expenses, must be considered when calculating the dynamic gearing, as these also impact the ratio.

Advantages	Disadvantages
• Considering the off-balance sheet liabilities and the cash flow from operations gives a significantly improved indicator	• No information on matching periods for financing
	• Actual borrowing costs are not considered
• Significantly improves comparison of companies	• May fluctuate heavily over time
• Is often used as key indicator in corporate management	

6.6   Working capital

Formula   **Sample calculation**

Current assets	6,888
− Cash and cash equivalents	(2,526)
− Current, non-interest bearing liablilities	(909)
= Working capital	**= 3,453**

Explanation

Working capital is defined as current assets less cash and cash equivalents
and less short-term, non-interest bearing liabilities (primarily trade payables).
It expresses the proportion of current assets working for a company (i.e., that
is generating sales), without generating capital costs in the closer sense of
the word. It is thus the portion of current assets with long-term financing.
The higher the working capital, the more secure the liquidity position. From
an analysts' perspective, negative working capital may be viewed positively,
as suppliers pre-finance the company's sales (especially retailers).

Advantages	Disadvantages
• Provides information on investment requirements when expanding capacity	• Non-optimum liquidity can lead to distortions
• Shows how strong the company's opportunities are to pass on costs to producers and suppliers	• The level of current assets disclosed can vary according to the use of various accounting options

6.7 Quick ratio

Formula

$$\frac{\text{Total current assets} - \text{Total inventory}}{\text{Total current liabilities}} \times 100\%$$

Sample calculation

$$\frac{6{,}888 - 2{,}016}{1{,}437 + 909 + 468} = \textbf{173.13\%}$$

Explanation

Liquidity indicators such as the quick ratio (also known as acid test) are often used for evaluating a company's creditworthiness. Bankers use this ratio to determine how quickly a company is able to pay off its current liabilities in case assets need to be converted into cash. This ratio differs from the current ratio in that it excludes inventory. The logic behind this is that while inventory may have been paid for and has value, it may not necessarily be converted into cash quickly. As a rule of thumb, the quick ratio should exceed 100%, thus current liabilities are covered by the company's cash position and its total receivables.

Advantages	Disadvantages
• Risk indicator if rule is not heeded	• Time-related, i.e., static figure
• Established in practice	• Too closely linked to balance sheet
• Serves to determine a company's creditworthiness	• Trade-off between liquidity and profitability
	• No consideration if total receivables can actually be collected

6.8   Current ratio

Formula

$$\frac{\text{Total current assets}}{\text{Total current liabilities}} \times 100\%$$

Sample calculation

$$\frac{6,888}{1,437 + 909 + 468} = \textbf{244.78\%}$$

Explanation

Liquidity indicators, such as the current ratio show the relationship between liquid assets to payment commitments. Liquid or current assets include cash and cash equivalents, marketable securities, total receivables and total inventory. The various ratios (also see quick ratio on the previous page) show the extent to which the current liabilities are covered by current assets. As a rule of thumb, the current ratio should total 200%, with a ratio of less than 100% being regarded as threatening the company's existence.

Advantages	Disadvantages
• Risk indicator if rule is not heeded	• Time-related, i.e., static figure
• Established in practice	• Too closely linked to balance sheet
• Rule of thumb for planning warehouses or credit control	• Trade-off between liquidity and profitability

6.9 Asset structure

Formula

$$\frac{\text{Fixed assets}}{\text{Current assets}} \times 100\%$$

Sample calculation

$$\frac{3{,}093}{6{,}888} \times 100\% = \textbf{44.90\%}$$

Explanation

The asset structure describes the relationship between fixed and current assets. This indicator shows a company's stability or flexibility, however typical asset structures in the respective industry should also be considered when reviewing this ratio.

A low asset structure can mean one of two things:

1. A low level of fixed assets allows a company to react more flexibly to changes on the market and fixed costs are lower due to the shorter capital lock-up period for all assets.
2. A company is working with assets that have already been written off. This allows us to assume that the technology used is out of date.

Advantages	Disadvantages
• Simple to calculate, as figures can be taken from balance sheet	• Inter-company comparisons are not particularly meaningful (in particular comparisons between various industries)
• Allows analysis over time as to whether the company is becoming more flexible	• Off-balance sheet assets (e.g., leasing) are not considered
• Allows assumptions to be made about capacity utilization and thus the earnings position: as a rule companies are more productive the more current assets there are per unit of fixed assets	• Disclosed goodwill can lead to distortions
	• Investment portfolios not used in operations reduce meaningfulness
	• Ratio is based on residual book values

6.10 Asset intensity

Formula

$$\frac{\text{Fixed assets}}{\text{Total assets}} \times 100\%$$

Sample calculation

$$\frac{3,093}{10,134} \times 100\% = \textbf{30.52\%}$$

Explanation

Asset intensity describes the relationship between fixed assets and total assets. The higher the asset intensity, the longer financial funds are locked up and, as a rule, the higher the associated fixed costs. The smaller this indicator, the less capital is tied-up over the long term. The indicator provides information on the company's ability to adapt to changing market conditions. When considering the asset intensity, the company's respective industry must also be considered. Asset intensity tends to be higher in particular in heavy industry (e.g., shipbuilding, engineering, cement, steel) and among utility companies. In these industries, a lower level of asset intensity could indicate out-of-date production methods as a result of assets already written off.

Advantages	Disadvantages
• Gives a rough indication of the flexibility of the company's operations and thus allows assumptions to be made about the financial and earnings stability:	• Impact of accounting policy cannot be avoided
	• High degree of intangible assets (e.g. goodwill) reduces meaningfulness
a) Material planning elasticity: the shorter the asset lock-up period, the higher the liquidity potential	• Meaningfulness significantly restricted for cross-industry company comparisons
b) Success elasticity: the shorter the asset lock-up, the lower the proportion of fixed costs	• Hidden assets lower asset intensity

6.11 Total current assets to total assets

Formula

$$\frac{\text{Total current assets}}{\text{Total assets}} \times 100\%$$

Sample calculation

$$\frac{6,888}{10,134} \times 100\% = \textbf{67.97\%}$$

Explanation

This indicator shows the ratio of total current assets to total assets. It shows the percentage of total capital which is locked-up in current assets. A high ratio is generally to be viewed positively, as current assets can be liquidated quickly. However, an extremely high ratio can indicate excessive stock levels, which push up warehousing costs. More detailed analysis of the current assets should cover the level of receivables and inventories in greater detail, as changes to the ratio of current to total assets are generally not due to chance.

Advantages	Disadvantages
• Provides information on the intensity of work	• Only the ratio of assets to revenues allows changes in asset structure indicators (e.g., asset intensity or ratio of current to total assets) to be interpreted, as assets alone do not generate any shareholder value
• Allows comparisons to be made between companies of the same size, same industry and same performance	
• Allows conditional assumptions to be made on the performance risk, i.e., how are the assets structured in order to use these to generate revenues	• The reason for changes cannot be seen, individual changes can counteract each other, which means that it is not possible to measure performance

6.12   Financial strength

Formula

$$\frac{\text{Cash flow from operating activities}}{\text{Payments for non-current assets}} \times 100\%$$

Sample calculation

$$\frac{1,248}{507} \times 100\% = \textbf{246.15\%}$$

Explanation

The financial strength indicator, also known as the self-financing ratio is calculated by contrasting the cash flow from operating activities with the additions to fixed assets, i.e., new, long-term investments. However, the term self-financing ratio is confusing, as, at the end of the day, all financing stems from outside the company (including revenues from operating activities).
The indicator thus shows whether an intended investment could be financed from the company's own financial strength. An indicator in excess of 100% shows that the company can finance the investment from its own cash flow, and can thus take decisions independently of the banks.

Advantages	Disadvantages
• Shows possible additional financing requirements for fixed investments • A differentiation can be made between maintenance and expansion investments	• May be subject to strong fluctuations over time • Limited meaningfulness for cross-industry comparisons

6.13 Reinvestment rate (II)

Formula

$$\frac{\text{Depreciation of property, plant, equipment, total}}{\text{Additions to property, plant, equipment, net}} \times 100\%$$

Sample calculation

$$\frac{402}{474} \times 100\% = \textbf{84.81\%}$$

Explanation

The reinvestment rate shows the amount of write-downs that were re-invested. If this figure is greater than 100%, depreciation for tangible assets was not fully reinvested in these assets. A figure of less than 100% shows that the company has invested in expansion. The lower the ratio, the higher the new investments of a company. Nonetheless, the industry and the composition of the tangible assets need to be considered, as both the time of useful life of fixed assets and a possible change in write-down methods (i.e., declining vs. linear) have an influence on the ratio.

Advantages	Disadvantages
• Allows maintenance investments to be analyzed	• Should always be considered in conjunction with any changes in efficiency
• Allows industry comparisons	
• As a rule, investments provide information on future profitability	• Can fluctuate heavily over time due to investment cycles
	• Inflation must also be considered for analysis over time
	• Increased use of leasing makes analysis more difficult

6.14 Depreciation rate

Formula

$$\frac{\text{Depreciation of property, plant and equipment}}{\text{Property, plant and equipment at year end}} \times 100\%$$

Sample calculation

$$\frac{402}{2,736} \times 100\% = \textbf{14.69\%}$$

Explanation

The depreciation rate usually shows the average useful life (in %) of the assets (the reverse figure shows the ratio in years). During comparison with other companies, the depreciation rate shows if a company's write-downs are in line with industry standards, or if it is aiming to disclose higher or lower profits. At the same time, a depreciation rate which increases over time shows that a company has had to make short-term replacement investments. In general, a high depreciation rate leads to lower useful lives for fixed assets, and thus to greater investments in subsequent years. This may be positive, as the company renews its fixed assets more quickly, and is thus more modern and competitive.

Advantages	Disadvantages
• Helpful in ascertaining a company's write-down policy	• Asset structure can be influenced (buy or lease)
• Allows comparison with competitors	• Distortions from assets written off in full respectively ascriptions
• Allows assumptions to be made on necessity of investments	• During high growth periods indicators may differ significantly
	• Change in composition of fixed assets can lead to distortions

6.15 Fixed assets to total equity

Formula

in the closer sense: $\dfrac{\text{Fixed assets}}{\text{Total equity}} \leq 1$

in the broader sense: $\dfrac{\text{Fixed assets}}{\text{Total equity + Long term debt and liabilities}} \leq 1$

Sample calculation

in the closer sense: $\dfrac{3{,}093}{5{,}493} = \mathbf{0.56}$

in the broader sense: $\dfrac{3{,}093}{5{,}493 + 288 + 1{,}140} = \mathbf{0.45}$

Explanation

This ratio demands that the capital lock-up period does not exceed the period for which the capital has been made available, i.e., that the assets tied into the company for the long-term are covered by long-term capital (in the closer sense exclusively by equity). If a company does not uphold this rule, the company may become forced to sell assets in order to service current liabilities.

Advantages	Disadvantages
• Shows the relationship between investment and financing	• Fixed assets do not necessarily require a long period to become liquid
• Solid, conservative indicator that is generally known and used	• Is rather an indicator for creditor protection
• Shows rule of matching periods	
• Risk indicator	

6.16 Golden financing rule

Formula

$$\frac{\text{Total current liabilities}}{\text{Total current assets}} \leq 1$$

$$\frac{\text{Total equity + Long-term liabilities}}{\text{Fixed assets}} \geq 1$$

Sample calculation

$$\frac{1{,}437 + 909 + 468}{6{,}888} = \textbf{0.41}$$

$$\frac{5{,}439 + 1{,}140 + 288}{3{,}093} = \textbf{2.24}$$

Explanation

These ratios state that the terms between obtaining and repaying capital on the one hand and the use of capital on the other should be in line with each other. According to this rule, capital may not be tied up in assets for a longer period than the capital is available to the company. If a company finances a long-term investment (e.g., a machine) with short-term financing, the loan may become due before the income required to repay the loan has been generated. This rule should be heeded in particular by young companies that depend on income from fewer products.

Advantages	Disadvantages
• Indicator helps to ensure that terms of assets and financing are in line	• Hidden assets are not taken into account
• Risk indicator for ability to fulfill payment commitments regarding time and value	• Not all current payment commitments are included on the balance sheet (wages and salaries)
• Indicator for company's future investment and financing policy	• Exact terms and the exact amount of income can thus not be seen on the balance sheet

6.17 Equity to assets ratio

Formula

$$\frac{\text{Total equity}}{\text{Fixed assets}} \times 100\%$$

$$\frac{\text{Total equity} + \text{Long-term liabilities}}{\text{Fixed assets}} \times 100\%$$

Sample calculation

$$\frac{5,493}{3,093} \times 100\% = \textbf{177.59\%}$$

$$\frac{5,493 + 1,140 + 288}{3,093} \times 100\% = \textbf{223.76\%}$$

Explanation

Indicator which shows how available capital is employed and which answers the question of the extent to which the fixed assets, which should be available to the company over the long term, are covered by equity that remains in the company for an equally long term. The higher the equity to assets ratio the better, as this means that parts of the current assets are also being financed long-term. The equity to assets ratio is thus the counterpart to the fixed assets to equity ratio. To the extent that it is known, in the second ratio the portion of current assets which has long-term financing can also be considered alongside the fixed assets (so-called staple inventory).

Advantages	Disadvantages
• Calculation shows whether principle of matching maturities is upheld	• Only a rough approximation is possible
• Serves as a control instrument to maintain a company's liquidity	• Existence of hidden assets leads to distortions
	• The type of fixed assets or quality is not considered

6.18   Current liabilities to sales

Formula

$$\frac{\text{Current liabilities}}{\text{Sales}} \times 100\%$$

Sample calculation

$$\frac{1,437 + 909 + 468}{14,019} \times 100\% = \textbf{20.07\%}$$

Explanation

This ratio shows what part of sales is due for repaying liabilities over the short term. The smaller this percentage, the more positive this is for the company. This key indicator should also be considered when analyzing companies' liquidity as liquid funds are generated by operations.

If we swap the numerator and the denominator (14,019/2,814=4.98), we obtain a factor which shows how often current liabilities were covered by revenues in this period. Expressed in days: 365/4.98=73.29 days. This means that the company needs approx. ten weeks to repay its current liabilities with sales (given straight-line revenue income). To improve meaningfulness, this figure can be compared to the duration of the operating cycle (also see inventory turnover, page 82).

Advantages	Disadvantages
• Overview of the relative amount of current liabilities	• Low meaningfulness
• Liquidity information on which portion of sales is left after repaying current liabilities	• Current liabilities depend on balance sheet date
• Is used during credit issuing process	• Cost structure is not taken into account

6.19 Receivables to short-term liabilities

Formula

$$\frac{\text{Receivables}}{\text{Short-term liabilities}} \times 100\%$$

Sample calculation

$$\frac{2,064}{1,437 + 909 + 468} \times 100\% = \textbf{73.35\%}$$

Explanation

Receivables to short-term liabilities shows to what extent short-term payables are covered by existing receivables. The ratio is, among others, an indicator for a company's ability to meet short-term financial obligations directly from its operating business (i.e., invoiced revenues).

In connection with this ratio the receivables turnover (see page 79) as well as the creditor's payment targets should be considered for the interpretation, because a high degree of short-term liabilities may also be an indicator for a strong market position. Should the ratio be less than 100%, the current ratio and quick ratio (see pages 93, 94) should also be taken into account for better assessing the danger of possible liquidity problems.

Advantages	Disadvantages
• Over time an indicator for a company's account receivables management respectively changes in payment targets	• Static ratio
	• No information on maturities
• Compares purchase to sales figures	• Especially for market dominating (retail) companies hardly meaningful
	• No general information provided if and for how long a company is still liquid

6.20   EBIT to short-term liabilities

Formula

$$\frac{\text{EBIT}}{\text{Short-term liabilities}} \times 100\%$$

Sample calculation

$$\frac{1,452}{1,437 + 909 + 468} \times 100\% = \textbf{51.60\%}$$

Explanation

This ratio compares a company's EBIT to short-term liabilities. It is an indicator for a company's ability to cover short-term liabilities through operating income. This is an important figure especially for creditors, as companies which are not able to meet short-term obligations will most likely struggle with long-term debt. This can have a strong effect on a company's ability for further leverage.

In the example above, the company would not be able to repay its total short-term liabilities through operating income. This may be an indicator for a company's structural problems, but again payment targets should be taken into account. If we change numerator and denominator, it becomes visible how many years it takes to repay the company's short-term debt (if necessary total liabilities can be compared) by operating income.

Advantages	Disadvantages
• High significance for a company's financial power, showing the actual debt release	• Solvency can only be determined by considering cash and cash equivalents
• Shows the ability to redeem short-term liabilities from the operating business	• Assets are not considered
	• Maturities are ignored
	• Cash flow is more meaningful than EBIT

6.21 EBIT interest coverage

Formula

$$\frac{\text{EBIT}}{\text{Interest expense (income), net operating}}$$

Sample calculation

$$\frac{1,452}{12} = \textbf{121.0}$$

Explanation

EBIT interest coverage shows the extent to which operating earnings cover interest expense. The lower this ratio, the higher the additional impact on earnings if the cost of debt increases, e.g., from a lower rating, and the lower the proportion of operating profit that can be distributed to shareholders.
On the other hand, a high interest coverage ratio indicates whether or not a company can take out further loans, which would lower the total cost of capital and thus increase the return on equity. In the example above the company shows relatively low net operating interest expense in the income statement leading to a very high EBIT interest coverage ratio.

Advantages	Disadvantages
• Shows risk for level of debt	• Should be considered in conjunction with other indicators (e.g., dynamic gearing), as not meaningful when taken alone
• Provides information on additional debt potential	
• Shows proportion of operating income that must be paid to repay debt	• Rental expense (leasing) is not considered
	• Little significance for companies with little or no debt

Chapter 7

Ratios for corporate valuation

7.1 Earnings per share (EPS), basic

Formula

Net income excl. extraordinary items − Preferred dividends
―――――――――――――――――――――――――――――――――――
Weighted average total common shares outstanding

Sample calculation

$$\frac{882 \pm 0 - 0}{\frac{(354 + 354)}{2}} = 2.49 \text{ per share}$$

Explanation

When calculating earnings per share, the company's profits (net income), adjusted for extraordinary items, are divided by the average number of total common shares outstanding.

This indicator is used most often to describe a company's performance over time and is one of the basics of company valuation. We must take into account the different ways of calculating net income depending on the various national accounting standards. Share options, convertible bonds, rights issues or capital increases raise the number of outstanding shares and thus dilute the earnings per share (also see page 112).

Advantages	Disadvantages
• Used in company valuations	• Static figure
• Large number of (analyst) estimates are freely accessible	• Net income may be subject to a wide range of adjustments
• Intuitive	• Calculations for the number of shares are not always uniform
• Used in industry comparisons	• Is subject to the greatest possible accounting policy latitude

7.2 Earnings per share (EPS), diluted

Formula

$$\frac{\text{Net income excl. extraordinary items} - \text{Preferred dividends} + \text{Interest expense for convertible bonds } (t-1)}{\text{Weighted average total common shares outstanding} + \text{Converted shares}}$$

Sample calculation

$$\frac{882 \pm 0 - 0 + 0}{\frac{354 + 354}{2} + 0} = \textbf{2.49 per share}$$

Explanation

In order to calculate diluted earnings per share, the company's profits (diluted net income), adjusted for extraordinary items and interest expense for convertible bonds, are divided by the average number of common shares including the new shares converted from convertible bonds. As soon as stock options or convertible bonds are converted into stocks, the number of total shares outstanding rises, which results in a negative impact on earnings per share, diluted.

This figure is the indicator used most often to describe a company's performance over time and is one of the basics of company valuation. We must take into account the different ways of calculating net income depending on the various national accounting standards. The difference between EPS, basic and diluted shows the impact of corporate actions (e.g. capital increase) and / or stock option plans.

Advantages	Disadvantages
• Used in company valuations	• Static figure
• Large number of (analyst) estimates are freely accessible	• Net income may be subject to a wide range of adjustments
• Adjusted earnings figure	• Calculations for the number of shares are not always uniform
• Used in industry comparisons	• Is subject to the greatest possible accounting policy latitude

7.3   Price earnings ratio (P / E)

Formula

$$\frac{\text{Price per share}}{\text{Earnings per share, diluted}}$$

Sample calculation

$$\frac{35.00}{2.49} = \mathbf{14.06}$$

Explanation

The P/E ratio expresses the factor by which the company's current profits are valued on the stock market. At the same time, a high P/E ratio can mean that the quality of profits in future years is increasing strongly and that the P/E ratio will decrease accordingly in the future.

However, as a company's profits are subject to major fluctuations, in particular in international comparisons, the meaning of the P/E ratio is limited. It is suitable for a quick comparison within one year and one industry. The long term P/E ratio for stocks (US market) is around 17. We thus often talk of overvaluation (P/E > 20) or undervaluation (P/E < 10) of the stock market. The P/E ratio is a highly volatile indicator that is strongly based on external expectations and influences.

Advantages	Disadvantages
• Allows quick comparison	• No consideration of company growth
• Non-industry dependent indicator	• Static indicator
• Easy to calculate	• Profits are dependent on accounting policy and national accounting standards and tax legislation
• Large number of profit estimates are freely accessible, making quick calculation possible	• A company must record profits to allow calculation of the P/E ratio

7.4 Price earnings growth ratio (PEG)

Formula

$$\frac{\text{P/E ratio}}{\text{Compounded average growth rate (CAGR)}}$$

Sample calculation

$$\frac{14.06}{10} = \mathbf{1.41}$$

Explanation

The price earnings growth ratio – or the dynamic P/E ratio – is the ratio of P/E to the company's compounded average growth rate. The CAGR is usually calculated for three to five years in the future.

This means that the price earnings growth ratio is mainly suitable for young, fast-growing companies and to some extent it puts the rigidity of the P/E ratio into perspective. For example, if a company records annual profit increases of 25% with a P/E ratio of 25, then this company would have a PEG ratio of 1 and would thus be, by definition, fairly valued. Companies with a PEG ratio > 1 are generally regarded as being overvalued, companies with PEG ratios < 1 tend to be undervalued.

Advantages	Disadvantages
• Easy to calculate	• Does not provide any clear criteria for the amount of the PEG ratio
• Tries to take a dynamic component into account	
• Used in relative comparisons	• Only marginally overcomes the disadvantages of the "traditional" P/E ratio

7.5 EBITDA per share

Formula

$$\frac{\text{EBITDA}}{\text{Total common shares outstanding}}$$

Sample calculation

$$\frac{1,944}{354} = \textbf{5.49}$$

Explanation

For calculating this ratio a company's EBITDA is compared to total common shares outstanding (diluted). The ratio shows a company's operating profit per share, not considering interest and taxes as well as depreciation and amortization. This cash flow approximation helps to internationally compare a company's earnings power within an industry, as national tax regulations, differences in the capital structure or depreciation policies are not taken into account.

Advantages	Disadvantages
• The impact of various forms of financing is not considered (may not apply to leasing)	• Only truly meaningful together with other indicators (e.g., enterprise value or market capitalization)
• Write-downs have no impact	• Cross-industry comparisons are difficult
• Can be used as indicator for a company's operative earnings power per share	
• Makes international comparison more simple, as national taxes are not included	

7.6   Cash flow per share

Formula

Cash flow from operating activities
$$\frac{\text{Cash flow from operating activities}}{\text{Total common shares outstanding}}$$

Sample calculation

$$\frac{1{,}248}{354} = \textbf{3.53}$$

Explanation

The cash flow per share is calculated by dividing the cash flow from operating activities by (diluted) common shares outstanding, respectively the average total common shares outstanding. Cash flow per share reflects the company's earnings power and is a valuable information in addition to EPS. In contrast to net income, the cash flow eliminates depreciation and amortization as well as changes in assets and liabilities. Therefore, the ratio is well-suited for company comparisons within the industry.

Advantages	Disadvantages
• Used in company valuations	• May vary strongly over time, as cash flow can fluctuate
• Allows relative peer group analyses	• Costs of capital respectively invested capital are not considered
• Cash flow is less susceptible to accounting policy	• Investment requirements are not taken into account

7.7 Market capitalization

Formula

Total common shares outstanding × Price per share

Sample calculation

354 mn × 35.00 = **12,390 mn**

Explanation

Market capitalization is given by the number of shares of a specific type, usually total common shares outstanding, multiplied by the respective share price. Market capitalization thus expresses the current market value of a company's equity.

As a rule, the higher a company's market capitalization the higher the investors' interest is, and thus the share's liquidity, i.e. the number of shares traded on a daily basis. Many stock exchanges use in particular the market capitalization and the daily volume as the decisive components for the company's membership of a stock index. If a company is included in an index (e.g., Dow Jones Industrial, FTSE 100, DAX), then this in turn increases awareness of the company among international investors.

Advantages	Disadvantages
• Used to compare company size • Market capitalization is often used to measure how investable shares are, i.e., lower market impact even for large-volume share orders	• There are various forms of market capitalization. A key factor is whether the shares are in "fixed hands" (e.g., family owned) or if they are freely available. The market capitalization in the indices are generally based on free float shares

7.8　Market capitalization to cash flow

Formula

$$\frac{\text{Market capitalization}}{\text{Cash flow from operating activities}}$$

Sample calculation

$$\frac{354 \times 35.00}{1,248} = \textbf{9.93}$$

Explanation

If we divide the share price by the cash flow per share, diluted, (alternatively market capitalization divided by operating cash flow as shown in the example above) then we obtain the company's price/cash flow ratio.

This indicator shows the factor by which the company's cash flow is valued on the stock market and serves as a supplement to the P/E ratio. The fact that the cash flow is more meaningful than profits allows us to derive the share's relative attractiveness compared to the industry by considering the price/cash flow ratio.

Advantages	Disadvantages
• Easy to calculate	• Investment requirements are not taken into account
• Cash flow is less susceptible to accounting policy	• Costs of capital are not considered
• Used in relative comparisons	• The underlying capital is not taken into account

7.9 Market capitalization to sales

Formula

Market capitalization
――――――――――
Sales

Sample calculation

$$\frac{12,390}{14,019} = \mathbf{0.88}$$

Explanation

This indicator is the ratio of the company's current stock market capitalization to its sales in the past fiscal year. It expresses the factor by which one unit of sales (i.e. one Euro) is valued on the stock market. For example, a ratio of 0.88 shows that 1.00 EUR of sales is currently valued at 0.88 EUR on the stock market.

It can be pertinent to use this indicator, for example, if a company does not record any profits and has to be compared within its industry. However, the indicator should always be observed in conjunction with the return on sales or sales growth, as its meaningfulness is otherwise limited.

Advantages	Disadvantages
• Used in company valuations	• Not precise enough to calculate a company's value
• Accounting policy has almost no impact	• Forms of financing are not taken into account
• Helpful if company does not yet record a positive operating result	• Different growth rates are not borne out
• Easy to calculate	

7.10 Price to book (total equity)

Formula

$$\frac{\text{Market capitalization}}{\text{Total equity}}$$

Sample calculation

$$\frac{12,390}{5,493} = \textbf{2.26}$$

Explanation

The price to book ratio shows the ratio of the current market capitalization divided by the balance sheet equity. The book value represents the quality of the company's assets. We must take into account that hidden assets may show book values which are significantly below their current fair value.

In general, a low price to book ratio indicates that a company is valued low. As a rule, the price to book ratio is greater 1, i.e., the shareholder pays a premium for the positive future prospects. During bear markets, the book value sometimes exceeds the respective share price. This holds particularly true for cyclical companies, for which profits slump more than average. However, these periods are mostly short-lived on the stock market.

Advantages	Disadvantages
• Easy to calculate	• Static indicator
• Used in company valuations	• Company growth is not taken into account
• Based on a company's quality	• Some national accounting laws allow goodwill to be offset against equity. This may lead to distortions

7.11   Net asset value per share

Formula

$$\frac{\text{Total equity} - \text{Preferred equity}}{\text{Total number of common shares outstanding}}$$

Sample calculation

$$\frac{5,493 - 0}{354} = \mathbf{15.52}$$

Explanation

The net asset value (NAV) per share, or also called book value per share is calculated by dividing total equity (minus preferred equity) by total common (respectively ordinary) shares outstanding. The result provides information on the company's net asset value. The higher the difference between the company's net asset value and the actual share price, the higher the amount of future free cash flows is already priced into the stock. This in turn means that stocks with relatively low net asset values in comparison to their share price may hold more risk for its investors in case cash flows fluctuate stronger than anticipated.

In case NAV is higher than the actual share price, this might be an indicator for implied risks which the company is facing (e.g., solvency problems, court decisions), which then again may threaten current levels of the company's equity.

Advantages	Disadvantages
• Easy to calculate	• Static indicator
• Used in company valuations, as it can show over- or under-valuation of a stock	• Company growth is not taken into account
• Helps to reveal company's quality	• Depending on accounting standards, sometimes goodwill may be offset against equity leading to distortions
• Risk indicator to a certain extent	

7.12 Enterprise value (EV)

Formula	Sample calculation
Market capitalization	12,390
− Cash and cash equivalents	(2,526)
+ Notes payable / short-term debt	2,814
+ Total long-term debt	1,428
+ Minority interest	36
+ Total preferred equity	0
= Enterprise value	**= 14,142**

Explanation

Enterprise value is given by adding the liabilities as well as minority interest and total preferred equity to a company's market value (market capitalization) and deducting the cash and equivalents. In contrast to the P/E ratio EV takes into account the capital structure as well as the (unprofitable) cash item in company comparisons. Calculations for the enterprise value are based on the idea that the company's financial structure does not impact its value.

At the end of the day, enterprise value shows the market value of the company's total capital and thus shows the company's value from the perspective of those providing capital (total investors and creditors).

Advantages	Disadvantages
• A larger proportion of invested capital (fund origin) is considered	• The book value of debt is simply an approximation of the actual amount of debt
• EV takes capital structure into account and "punishes" companies with high cash levels	• Complex calculation if market capitalization is not known

7.13   Enterprise value / EBIT

Formula

$$\frac{\text{Enterprise value}}{\text{EBIT}}$$

Sample calculation

$$\frac{14,142}{1,452} = \mathbf{9.74}$$

Explanation

EV/EBIT compares a company's market value to its operating profits. This indicator thus offers an alternative to the P/E ratio, as it takes into account different financing structures and taxation at an international level by removing interest charges and tax expense from net income. In the example above, EV/EBIT ratio of 9.74 puts the P/E ratio of more than 14 (also see page 113) into perspective.

Advantages	Disadvantages
• Independent of form of financing	• Costs of capital are not taken into account
• National tax rate does not have any impact	• Investment requirements are not borne out
• Offers a valuation of the operating result	

7.14   Enterprise value / EBITDA

Formula

Enterprise value
EBITDA

Sample calculation

$$\frac{14,142}{1,944} = \mathbf{7.27}$$

Explanation

EV/EBITDA is the ratio of a company's enterprise value to its operating earnings before interest, taxes, depreciation and amortization (EBITDA). This indicator shows how often the operating income is included in the company's value (in this case more than seven times). In a similar fashion to EV/EBIT this ratio is superior to the traditional P/E ratio, as it also eliminates the various write-down modalities in addition to various financing structures and taxes, which means that company's can be compared internationally within the same industry.

Advantages	Disadvantages
• Allows international comparisons	• Costs of capital are not taken into account
• Helpful when valuing companies that do not yet generate any profits	• Strategic investments are not considered
• Is a commonly used indicator among financial analysts	• Does not allow any conclusions to be drawn about a company's ability to manage the necessary operating assets (net current assets)
	• Investment requirements are not considered

7.15   Pay out ratio

Formula

$$\frac{\text{Dividends paid}}{\text{Net income}} \times 100\%$$

Sample calculation

$$\frac{354}{882} \times 100\% = \textbf{40.14\%}$$

Explanation

The pay out ratio describes which portion of net income was distributed to shareholders. There are only two possibilities for net income:

- it is reinvested or,
- it is paid out to shareholders.

A company's pay out ratio is primarily influenced by a company's self-financing requirements, the shareholder's tax situation and the shareholder's yield requirements. The more profitable a company, the higher the reinvestment ratio should be and the lower the corresponding pay out ratio.

Advantages	Disadvantages
• Shows an investor's actual cash return	• Profits are a must
• A high pay out ratio can serve as collateral for an investment	• Can vary over time
• The amount of retained profits can be calculated using the pay out ratio, which in turn allows conclusions to be drawn about the additional financing requirements with the given investment requirements	

7.16   Dividend per share

Formula

$$\frac{\text{Total dividends paid}}{\text{Total common shares outstanding}}$$

Sample calculation

$$\frac{354}{354} = 1.00$$

Explanation

The dividend per share is calculated by dividing the total cash dividends paid to shareholders by the total primary shares outstanding. Dividends are either distributed to shareholders on a quarterly or annual basis. On the day of distribution the dividend is deducted from the share price and reflects the interest of a share investment (also see dividend yield on page 127). By comparing the dividend per share to its actual share price the interest can be compared to other peer group companies for evaluating a company's attractiveness.

Advantages	Disadvantages
• Dividend per share serves as an additional criteria for determining a company's attractiveness	• Dividend financing is not taken into account, i.e. is it paid from net income or retained earnings
• Used for the security aspect of an investment	• Dividends itself do not express a yield
	• Dividends can vary strongly over time

7.17 Dividend yield

Formula

$$\frac{\text{Dividend per share}}{\text{Share price}} \times 100\%$$

Sample calculation

$$\frac{1.00}{35.00} \times 100\% = \textbf{2.86\%}$$

Explanation

The dividend yield is given by the ratio of dividend per share to the price per share. It shows the effective interest rate for the capital invested in shares. The dividend yield is particularly important, especially for comparisons with other forms of investment such as bonds. However, investors must take into account the fact that dividend payments are much less certain than coupon payments for bonds. At the same time the dividends are subtracted from the share price on the day the dividends are distributed, which must be compensated for over time by an increase in the share price.

Advantages	Disadvantages
• The dividend yield can also be used as an additional criterion for a company's attractiveness	• Dividend financing is not taken into account
• Used to determine relative attractiveness	• Can only be calculated if dividends are paid
• Used for the security aspect of an investment	• There is no "optimum" dividend yield
	• Individual investor's yield depends on the share price on purchase date

7.18 Beta

Formula

> Co-variance of share A to benchmark B
> (Volatility of benchmark B)^2

Sample calculation

As a result of numerous factors to be considered for calculating beta, we have not included a sample calculation. A beta of 0.9 has been assumed for the following sample calculations.

Explanation

Beta measures a share's volatility compared to an index during a certain period in the past (e.g., 90 or 200 days). If beta is 0.9, the share price has increased by 9% if the index increased by 10% during this period. This also applies accordingly if the index falls.

The higher a company's beta, the higher the volatility and thus the risk for an investor. One of investor relations' aims is to keep beta as low as possible by up-to-the-minute, in-depth communication. Beta is, in turn, of key importance when calculating the costs of equity or option premiums. The higher the costs of capital (also see WACC page 131), the lower the company's value using the DCF method.

Advantages	Disadvantages
• Is regarded as a measure of risk	• Based on past figures
• Calculations for the costs of equity (CAPM) are often based on beta	• Can vary strongly over time
	• Depends on time horizon selected

7.19 Cost of equity

Formula

Risk-free interest rate + (Market risk premium × Beta)

Sample calculation

4.50% + (3.50% × 0.9) = **7.65%**

Explanation

The cost of equity forms the basis for various calculation models (e.g., discounted cash flow, economic value added) when valuing companies. As equity generally does not generate any direct costs, the cost of equity may be regarded as imputed opportunity costs, i.e., it is the minimum return that could have been generated with the same capital by making other investments.

Long-term government bonds are taken to represent the risk-free interest rate (e.g., 10 Year Government Bond Euroland). The market risk premium is the anticipated additional return from other forms of investment, such as shares. The long-term share return is approx. 8.00%, the risk-free interest rate is approx. 4.50%. This means that the average market risk premium adds up to approx. 3.50%. Multiplying this figure with beta plus the risk-free interest rate provides the cost of equity according to the so-called capital asset pricing model (CAPM).

Advantages	Disadvantages
• Is often used in valuing companies	• A one-factor-model
• Components are simple to explain	• Basis for calculations (index) is not uniform for the market risk premium
• Used for calculating the total costs of capital	• Beta is based on the past
	• Beta depends strongly on the underlying period

7.20 Cost of debt

Formula

> (Risk-free interest rate + Corporate bond spread) × (1 − Tax rate)
>
> **or (if no rating is available):**
>
> $$\frac{\sum (\text{Long term debt} \times \text{Interest rate})}{\sum \text{Long term debt}} \times (1 - \text{Tax rate})$$

Sample calculation

$$(4.50\% + 0.30\%) \times \left(1 - \frac{594}{1,497} \right) = \mathbf{2.90\%}$$

Explanation

Two methods are used to calculate costs of debt:
If a company has a rating, to calculate the costs of debt analysts calculate the risk-free interest rate (in the Euro-zone generally, for example, the 10 Year Government Bond Euroland, in the US the 10 Year Treasuries) plus the corporate bond spread (risk premium for company bonds), which is derived from the rating and which changes daily depending on the market environment.

However, the costs of debt can also be calculated using an alternate method. For this purpose, the individual credit totals are multiplied by the respective interest rate and divided by total credit. This shows the weighted borrowing rate. For both calculations we must consider the tax effect (interest payments reduce profit and thus reduce taxation).

Advantages	Disadvantages
• Tax effect taken into account	• Hard to calculate if no rating is available
• Can be a component of calculations for total costs	• The respective interest rates for individual credits are not available
• The actual costs of debt are taken into account	• Company's financial risk is reflected only very imprecisely by this figure

7.21 Weighted average cost of capital (WACC)

Formula

$$\left(\frac{\text{Total equity}}{\text{Total equity} + \text{Interest-bearing debt}} \right) \times \text{Cost of equity}$$

$$+ \left(\frac{\text{Interest-bearing debt}}{\text{Total equity} + \text{Interest-bearing debt}} \right) \times \text{Cost of debt}$$

Sample calculation

$$\left(\frac{5,493}{5,493 + 1,896} \times 7.65\% \right)$$

$$+ \left(\frac{1,896}{5,493 + 1,896} \times 2.90\% \right) = \mathbf{6.43\%}$$

Explanation

WACC (Weighted average cost of capital) is the most wide-spread discount factor on the capital markets used to calculate a company's value. In order to weight the capital costs correctly, as a rule only the interest-bearing liabilities (i.e., no provisions) and the balance sheet equity (alternatively: market capitalization) are used.

WACC has a material impact on the company's value in both the discounted cash flow method as well as in the EVA model. As a rule, WACC is between 5% and 10% according to capital structure and industry. In the case of high-growth companies, the higher risk premium can mean that WACC is higher than 10%.

Advantages	Disadvantages
• Used as a discount factor in company valuations	• Indicator oriented towards the past
• Shows minimum return on capital invested (cf. ROIC)	• No uniform method of calculation
• Overcomes disadvantages that are inherent in solely examining interest expense	• Indicator often manipulated

7.22 Discounted cash flow method (DCF)

Formula

$$\sum_{t=1}^{n} \frac{\text{Free cash flow}_t}{(1 + \text{WACC})^t} + \frac{\text{Terminal value}_n}{(1 + i)^{n-1}}$$

Sample calculation

$$\frac{851.40}{(1 + 0.0643)} + \frac{936.54}{(1+0.0643)^2} + \frac{1,030.19}{(1 + 0.0643)^3} + \frac{1,133.21}{(1 + 0.0643)^4}$$

$$+ \frac{1,246.53}{(1 + 0.0643)^5} + \frac{\dfrac{1,246.53}{0.0643}}{(1 + 0.0643)^5} = 4,277.29 + 14,196.18 = \mathbf{18,473.47}$$

Explanation

The discounted cash flow method calculates the current value of the company by adding the present values of cash flows from coming years. In the simplified model, the free cash flows for the coming years are explicitly estimated and discounted (here: 10% increase in annual free cash flow based on year 2, cf. page 54). In order to calculate the terminal value, constant cash flows (without further growth) are assumed for all further years and these are also discounted. The sum of the discounted cash flows and the terminal value then results in the company's value. For calculating the equity value the market value of debt capital needs to be deducted. A problem in the DCF method is estimating the future cash flows and correct selection of the discount factor (as a rule the so-called WACC).

Advantages	Disadvantages
• Used for company valuations	• Very complex
• Overcomes disadvantages that are inherent in purely observing multiples	• The terminal value has a sustained influence on the total value of the company
• Highly variable corporate valuation concept	• Company value can be easily impacted by manipulation (or incorrect estimates) of the capital costs

7.23 Economic value added (EVA)

Formula

(ROIC − WACC) × Invested capital

Sample calculation

$(11.52\% - 6.43\%) \times 7{,}389 = \mathbf{376.10}$

Explanation

Economic value added (EVA) is based on the idea that a company only generates value for investors if the return on invested capital exceeds the company's underlying capital costs. This excess return multiplied with the invested capital shows the annual increase or decrease in value of a company. In the above example, the EVA in year 2 would be 376.10 million, which ceteris paribus should be reflected in an increase in market capitalization by this amount over time.

EVA should always be used together with a pure observation of the cash flow, because although a company generates positive cash flows, it may still be destroying value and have a negative EVA.

Advantages	Disadvantages
• In contrast to the cash flow, a company's value generation or destruction can be calculated on an annual basis • Overcomes traditional problems with multiples valuation	• Large number of adjustments possible • Not reasonable in an environment with high inflation tendencies • EVA should always be considered over time • It is possible that participating interests that may have been acquired from an operational perspective, but which are not fully consolidated are not taken into account

7.24 Market value added (MVA)

Formula

$$\sum_{t=1}^{t=\infty} \frac{EVA_t}{(1 + WACC)^t}$$

MVA = Enterprise value − (Total equity + Total long-term debt & liabilities)

Sample calculation

14,142 − (5,493 + 1,140 + 288) = **7,221**

Explanation

Market value added corresponds to the difference between the current value of the company (enterprise value or, alternatively, market capitalization plus net debt) and the balance sheet value of the long-term capital. As a result, market value added shows the amount that the market is prepared to pay over and above the available balance sheet capital. This means that MVA corresponds to the sum of the discounted current annual EVAs.

This indicator thus shows the accumulated amount by which the company or the management has increased the shareholder value over time.

Advantages	Disadvantages
• International, cross-industry comparability	• MVA is only suitable for listed companies
• Attaches a value to management performance	• MVA depends on the total market

Literature

Benzel, W., Wolz, E.	»Bilanzanalyse für Aktionäre«, 2nd Edition, Walhalla Fachverlag, Regensburg/Berlin, 2000
Bussiek, J., Fraling, R., Hesse, K.	»Unternehmensanalyse mit Kennzahlen«, Gabler-Verlag, Wiesbaden, 1993
DATEV eG	»Tabellen und Informationen für den steuerlichen Berater«, DATEV eG Nürnberg, 2003
Deutsches Steuerberaterinstitut e.V.	»Steuerberater Handbuch 2002/03«, Stollfuß Verlag, Bonn, 2002
Gabler	»Gabler Wirtschafts-Lexikon«, 14th Edition, Gabler Verlag, Wiesbaden, 1997
Kruschwitz, L.	»Investitionsrechnung«, 9th Edition, Oldenbourg Verlag, München, 2003
Knief, P.	»Steuerberater und Wirtschaftsprüfer Jahrbuch 2003«, 21st Edition, Deutscher Sparkassen Verlag GmbH, Stuttgart, 2002
Olfert, K.	»Finanzierung«, 8th Edition, Kiehl Verlag, Ludwigshafen, 1994
Olfert, K.	»Investition«, 9th Edition, Kiehl Verlag, Ludwigshafen, 2003
Online	www.ifrs-portal.com, February 2005
Ossola-Haring, C.	»Das große Handbuch Kennzahlen zur Unternehmensführung«, Verlag Moderne Industrie, Landsberg/Lech, 1999
Perridon, L., Steiner, M.	»Finanzwirtschaft der Unternehmung«, 10th Edition, Verlag Vahlen, München, 1999
Siegwart, H.	»Kennzahlen für die Unternehmensführung«, 6th Edition, Verlag Paul Haupt, Bern, 2002
Wöhe, G.	»Einführung in die Betriebswirtschaftslehre«, 18th Edition, Verlag Vahlen, München, 1993

Imprint

1st Edition

Idea:

Michael Diegelmann

Conception:

Michael Diegelmann
Ulrich Wiehle

Authors & Editorial Staff:

Ulrich Wiehle
Michael Diegelmann
Henryk Deter
Dr. Peter Noel Schömig
Michael Rolf

Cover Design:

cometis AG

Project Management:

Michael Diegelmann
Ulrich Wiehle

Responsibility:

cometis AG
Unter den Eichen 7
65195 Wiesbaden
Germany

Tel: +49 (0)611/20 58 55-0
Fax: +49 (0)611/20 58 55-66
E-mail: info@cometis.de
www.cometis.de
www.cometis-publishing.de

Exemplary excerpt

100 IFRS Financial Ratios
Dictionary German / English

EBIT

Formula	Sample calculation
Net income	882
± Extraordinary items	0
+ Minority interest	21
+ Taxes	594
± Financial result	(45)
= **EBIT**	**= 1,452**

Explanation

EBIT stands for "earnings before interest and taxes". In the US the ratio is also known as operating income/operating profit. It is generally used to assess the company's earnings position, in particular in international comparisons. However, EBIT is not only pure earnings before interest and taxes as it is referred to by many people, but in more precise terms it is the operating result before the financial and thus investment result, which may have a major impact on the pre-tax earnings depending on the respective company. EBIT can also be calculated by subtracting total operating expenses from sales (incl. other operating income).

Advantages	Disadvantages
• Allows assumptions to be made about pure operating activities	• Only meaningful when considered together with other indicators (e.g., revenues)
• Industry-wide comparisons of operating income are possible, in particular when other ratios are also considered (e.g., revenues)	• Interest income, which may not be included in EBIT, can be part of operating income (income from financing activities, e.g., financing installments)
• Distortions from tax effects are not included	
• Used internationally	

EBIT

Formel   **Rechenbeispiel**

Jahresüberschuss	882
± Außerordentliches Ergebnis	0
+ Minderheiten	21
+ Steuern	594
± Finanzergebnis	− 45
= EBIT	**= 1.452**

Erläuterung

EBIT steht für »Earnings before interest and taxes«. In den USA wird die Kennzahl EBIT als Operating income bezeichnet. Dieses operative Ergebnis vor Zinsen und Steuern wird gewöhnlich für die Beurteilung der Ertragssituation des Unternehmens, insbesondere im internationalen Vergleich herangezogen. Jedoch ist das EBIT nicht nur das reine Ergebnis vor Zinsen und Steuern, wie es weitläufig bezeichnet wird, sondern genauer gesagt das operative Ergebnis vor dem Finanz- und damit Beteiligungsergebnis, was je nach Unternehmen großen Einfluss auf den Gewinn vor Steuern haben kann. Das EBIT kann alternativ auch berechnet werden, indem von den Umsätzen (inkl. sonstiger betrieblicher Erträge) alle operativen Kosten abgezogen werden.

Vorteile	Nachteile
• Lässt Rückschlüsse auf das reine operative Geschäft zu	• Nur in Bezug zu anderen Kennzahlen (z.B. Umsätze) aussagefähig
• Insbesondere unter Zuhilfenahme anderer Kennzahlen (z.B. Umsätze) werden industrieweite Vergleiche der operativen Ergebnisse ermöglicht	• Auch Zinseinkünfte, die keine Berücksichtigung im EBIT finden (Einkünfte aus Finanzierungstätigkeit, z.B. Ratenfinanzierungen) können Bestandteil des operativen Einkommens sein
• Verzerrungen durch steuerliche Einflüsse bleiben außen vor	
• Findet international Anwendung	

Publications

Wiehle, Diegelmann, Deter, Dr. Schömig, Rolf

100 IFRS Financial Ratios
Dictionary German/English

Wiesbaden, 2005, 2nd Edition
ISBN: 3-9809461-2-6

Our Dictionary will soon be available in other languages:

- **English / French**
- **English / Spanish**
- **English / Italian**
- **German / French**

All versions will be available as US GAAP or IFRS edition.

If you are interested to find out more about our innovative products, please get in touch with us.

Contact:
cometis AG
Henryk Deter
Unter den Eichen 7
65195 Wiesbaden
Germany

Tel: +49 (0)611/20 58 55-0
Fax: +49 (0)611/20 58 55-66
E-mail: deter@cometis.de
www.cometis-publishing.de